Careers in Focus

EDUCATION

THIRD EDITION

Ferguson

An imprint of Infobase Publishing

Careers in Focus: Education, Third Edition

Copyright © 2009 by Infobase Publishing

Ferguson
An imprint of Infobase Publishing
132 West 31st Street
New York NY 10001

Library of Congress Cataloging-in-Publication Data

Careers in focus. Education. — 3rd ed.
    p. cm.
 Includes bibliographical references and index.
 ISBN-13: 978-0-8160-7298-9 (alk. paper)
 ISBN-10: 0-8160-7298-1 (alk. paper)
 1. Education—Vocational guidance—United States—Juvenile literature. 2. Teaching—Vocational guidance—United States—Juvenile literature. I. Ferguson Publishing. II. Title: Education.
 LB1775.2.C37 2009
 370.23'73—dc22

                          2008034823

Ferguson books are available at special discounts when purchased in bulk quantities for businesses, associations, institutions, or sales promotions. Please call our Special Sales Department in New York at (212) 967-8800 or (800) 322-8755.

You can find Ferguson on the World Wide Web at http://www.fergpubco.com

Text design by David Strelecky
Cover design by Salvatore Luongo

Printed in the United States of America

IBT MSRF 10 9 8 7 6 5 4 3 2

This book is printed on acid-free paper.

Table of Contents

Introduction

The majority of people involved in education are teachers. Teaching responsibilities can vary greatly from job to job in terms of subjects, schedules, and assigned duties. For example, elementary school teachers typically work with one group of children all day, while secondary school teachers (junior and senior high school) meet four, five, or more groups of students throughout the day. College professors may only present a few lectures per day, but many must also conduct scholarly research.

Teachers of younger children perform many of the roles of a parent, so the jobs of the preschool, kindergarten, and elementary school teachers include the personal and social responsibilities that are assumed by parents at home. These jobs, of course, also include the full gamut of responsibilities for the emotional and intellectual growth of children. Responsibilities of teachers of grades K–6 include teaching, selecting and planning coursework, grading homework, and evaluating student achievement. These teachers also participate in conferences with parents, other teachers, and administrators, on issues involving curriculum, instruction, and guidance.

High school teachers' basic responsibilities are similar to those of elementary school teachers, but they act less as parent substitutes and are more concerned with academics. Typically, high school teachers specialize in one or two subjects. But even at the high school level, teachers are concerned about more than the students' academic progress. They also help students deal with personal problems and advise them in matters concerning their future, such as selecting colleges and careers.

Similar to the high school teacher, the college professor shares a commitment to a specific field of knowledge, but the commitment is generally more specific and intensive. College professors generally participate in the activities of a professional society or association, and most write and publish books and articles to advance in their careers. Increasingly, professors are sought out as consultants in business, government, and public service. With more demands on their time extending outside of the classroom, college teachers may find difficulty in spending as much time with students as they would like. Professors with years of experience and a high level of specialization may choose to teach at the graduate level. These teachers spend more time in research activities and work with a small number of graduate students.

At all levels of the profession, teachers today are generally better educated than they were in the past. All states require the minimum of a bachelor's degree for a beginning position, and many teachers have graduate degrees.

A variety of new opportunities for educators have evolved in nontraditional areas. Qualified education professionals are needed to work in agencies such as adult education programs, recreation departments, drug and alcohol abuse programs, Planned Parenthood units, and government organizations such as the Peace Corps and Job Corps. Careers in education extend beyond the typical classroom setting.

Thousands of people are employed by professional organizations, private agencies with educational programs, and government offices of education. Every state in the United States has an office of education that hires professionals to monitor and make recommendations for local school policies. The federal government also employs professionals to ensure that legislative mandates regarding education are carried out at the state and local levels. Federal education officials are concerned with such areas as bilingual education, transportation, and school health.

Colleges and universities hire workers with a background in education to work as administrators. These workers handle financial aid distribution, record-keeping, course development, and hiring.

Most positions in education outside the classroom require teaching experience. For example, school and college administrators, including superintendents and principals, often first serve as teachers. Association leaders and educators in government offices also often begin their careers as teachers. To be qualified and experienced for these higher-level positions, most education administrators and government officials have also completed graduate study in education.

According to the U.S. Department of Labor, employment in the field of education is expected to increase by 11 percent between 2006 and 2016, about as fast as the average growth rate projected for all industries combined. Many job openings will arise from the need to replace workers who retire or change occupations.

The fastest growing careers in the education industry include adult and vocational education teachers, college and university professors and administrators, computer trainers, elementary school teachers, and nursing instructors. The employment of career counselors, guidance counselors, preschool and kindergarten teachers, school administrators, and teacher aides is expected to grow at an average rate. In addition, enrollment by foreign students has been growing rapidly in recent years, spurring demand for specialized educators such as English as a second language teachers, as well as interpreters and translators.

Anticipated growth in this industry is due, for the most part, to two major trends. First, the number of people attending college (including adults returning to school to continue their education) is expected to grow in the next decade. At the same time, the federal government has become committed to lowering the number of students per class to improve educational environments, increasing the need for more teachers.

Though college enrollment is also expected to increase, competition for full-time faculty and administrator positions will remain high. Lower paid, part-time instructors, such as visiting professors and graduate students, are increasingly replacing tenure-track faculty positions.

The U.S. Department of Labor projects that the number of special education teachers will grow faster than average over the next several years because of increasing enrollment of special education students, continued emphasis on inclusion of disabled students in general education classrooms, and the effort to reach students with problems at younger ages.

Each article in *Careers in Focus: Education* discusses a particular education occupation in detail. The articles also appear in Ferguson's *Encyclopedia of Careers and Vocational Guidance*, but have been updated and revised with the latest information from the U.S. Department of Labor and other sources.

The following paragraphs detail the sections and features that appear in the book.

The **Quick Facts** section provides a brief summary of the career including recommended school subjects, personal skills, work environment, minimum educational requirements, salary ranges, certification or licensing requirements, and employment outlook. This section also provides acronyms and identification numbers for the following government classification indexes: the Dictionary of Occupational Titles (DOT), the Guide for Occupational Exploration (GOE), the National Occupational Classification (NOC) Index, and the Occupational Information Network (O*NET)-Standard Occupational Classification System (SOC) index. The DOT, GOE, and O*NET-SOC indexes have been created by the U.S. government; the NOC index is Canada's career classification system. Readers can use the identification numbers listed in the Quick Facts section to access further information about a career. Print editions of the DOT (*Dictionary of Occupational Titles*. Indianapolis, Ind.: JIST Works, 1991) and GOE (*Guide for Occupational Exploration*. Indianapolis, Ind.: JIST Works, 2001) are available at libraries.

Electronic versions of the NOC (http://www23.hrdc-drhc.gc.ca) and O*NET-SOC (http://online.onetcenter.org) are available on the Internet. When no DOT, GOE, NOC, or O*NET-SOC numbers are present, this means that the U.S. Department of Labor or Human Resources Development Canada have not created a numerical designation for this career. In this instance, you will see the acronym "N/A," or not available.

The **Overview** section is a brief introductory description of the duties and responsibilities involved in this career. Oftentimes, a career may have a variety of job titles. When this is the case, alternative career titles are presented. Employment statistics are also provided, when available. The **History** section describes the history of the particular job as it relates to the overall development of its industry or field. **The Job** describes the primary and secondary duties of the job. **Requirements** discusses high school and postsecondary education and training requirements, any certification or licensing that is necessary, and other personal requirements for success in the job. **Exploring** offers suggestions on how to gain experience in or knowledge of the particular job before making a firm educational and financial commitment. The focus is on what can be done while still in high school (or in the early years of college) to gain a better understanding of the job. The **Employers** section gives an overview of typical places of employment for the job. **Starting Out** discusses the best ways to land that first job, be it through the college career services office, newspaper ads, Internet employment sites, or personal contact. The **Advancement** section describes what kind of career path to expect from the job and how to get there. **Earnings** lists salary ranges and describes the typical fringe benefits. The **Work Environment** section describes the typical surroundings and conditions of employment—whether indoors or outdoors, noisy or quiet, social or independent. Also discussed are typical hours worked, any seasonal fluctuations, and the stresses and strains of the job. The **Outlook** section summarizes the job in terms of the general economy and industry projections. For the most part, Outlook information is obtained from the U.S. Bureau of Labor Statistics and is supplemented by information gathered from professional associations. Job growth terms follow those used in the *Occupational Outlook Handbook*. Growth described as "much faster than the average" means an increase of 21 percent or more. Growth described as "faster than the average" means an increase of 14 to 20 percent. Growth described as "about as fast as the average" means an increase of 7 to 13 percent. Growth described as "more slowly than the average" means an increase of 3 to 6 percent. "Little or no change" means a decrease of 2 percent to an increase of 2 percent. "Decline" means a decrease of 3 percent or more. Each article ends with **For More Information,** which lists organizations that provide information on training, education, internships, scholarships, and job placement.

Careers in Focus: Education also includes photographs, informative sidebars, and interviews with professionals in the field.

Although the basic goal of the education field—the transmission and creation of knowledge—has remained unchanged for centuries, the nature and variety of educational careers has changed, and will continue to change, immensely over the years. The field of education presents some of the most challenging and rewarding careers available, and this book can help you realize how your skills and talents might translate into a promising educational profession.

Adult and Vocational Education Teachers

OVERVIEW

Adult and vocational education teachers teach basic academic subjects to adults who did not finish high school or who are new to speaking English. They help prepare post-high school students and other adults for specific occupations and provide personal enrichment. Adult education teachers offer basic education courses, such as reading and writing, or continuing education courses, such as literature and music. Vocational education teachers offer courses designed to prepare adults for specific occupations, such as data processor or automobile mechanic. Approximately 261,000 teachers of adult literacy, remedial, and self-enrichment education are employed in the United States.

HISTORY

During colonial times in America, organized adult education was started to help people make up for schooling missed as children or to help people prepare for jobs. Apprenticeships were an early form of vocational education in the American colonies, wherein individuals were taught a craft by working with a skilled person in a particular field. For example, a young boy might agree to work for a printer for five to 10 years and at the end of that time be able to open up his own printing business. Training programs continued to develop as carpenters, bricklayers, and other craftspeople learned their skills through vocational training.

Peak periods in adult education typically occurred during times of large-scale immigration. Evening schools filled with foreign-born

QUICK FACTS

School Subjects
English
Psychology
Speech

Personal Skills
Communication/ideas
Helping/teaching

Work Environment
Primarily indoors
Primarily one location

Minimum Education Level
Bachelor's degree

Salary Range
$24,610 to $43,910 to
$75,680+

Certification or Licensing
Required by certain states

Outlook
Much faster than the average

DOT
N/A

GOE
12.03.02

NOC
4131

O*NET-SOC
25-3011.00, 25-3021.00

persons eager to learn the language and culture of their new home and to prepare for the tests necessary for citizenship.

In 1911, Wisconsin established the first State Board of Vocational and Adult Education in the country, and in 1917 the federal government supported the continuing education movement by funding vocational training in public schools for individuals over the age of 14. Immediately after World War II, the federal government took another large stride in financial support of adult and vocational education by creating the G.I. Bill of Rights, which provided money for veterans to pursue further job training.

Today colleges and universities, vocational high schools, private trade schools, private businesses, and other organizations offer adults the opportunity to prepare for a specific occupation or pursue personal enrichment. More than 20 million people in the United States take advantage of this opportunity each year, creating many jobs for teachers in this field.

THE JOB

Adult and vocational education courses take place in a variety of settings, including high schools, universities, religious institutions, and businesses. The responsibilities of an adult or vocational education teacher are similar to those of a school teacher and include planning and conducting lectures, supervising the use of equipment, grading homework, evaluating students, writing and preparing reports, and counseling students.

Adult education is divided into two main areas: basic education and continuing education. Basic education includes reading, writing, and mathematics courses and is designed for adult students who have not finished high school. Many of these students are taking basic education courses to earn the equivalent of a high school diploma (the General Equivalency Diploma, or GED). Some high school graduates who received poor grades in high school also enroll in basic education classes before attending a four-year college. Recent immigrants may take basic education classes to learn to read, write, and do arithmetic in the language of their new country.

Unlike basic education, continuing education for adults is aimed at students who have finished high school or college and are taking courses for personal enrichment. Class topics might include creative writing, art appreciation, photography, history, and a host of other subjects. Often businesses will enroll employees in continuing education courses as part of job training to help them develop computer skills, learn to write grant proposals, or become convincing public

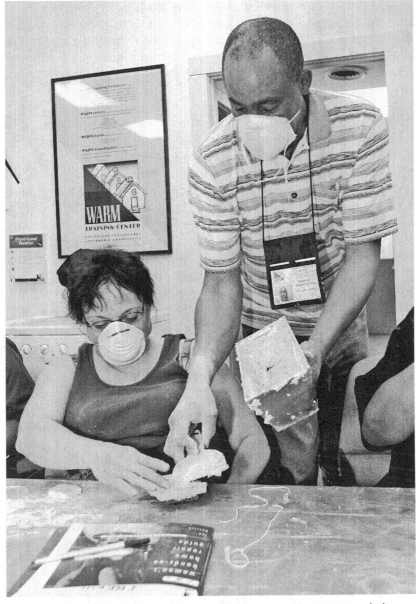

A vocational education instructor teaches a drywall repair workshop.
(Jim West Photography)

speakers. Sometimes, businesses will hire an adult education teacher to come into the business to train employees on-site. These continuing education teachers are called *training representatives*.

Vocational education teachers prepare students for specific careers that do not require college degrees, such as cosmetologist, chef, or welder. They demonstrate techniques and then advise the students as they attempt these techniques. They also lecture on the class subject and direct discussion groups. Instruction by a vocational education teacher may lead to the student's certification, so teachers may follow a specific course plan approved by an accrediting association. They may also be involved in directing a student to an internship and local job opportunities.

Whether teaching in a basic education or continuing education classroom, adult and vocational education teachers work with small groups of students. In addition to giving lectures, they assign textbooks and homework assignments. They prepare and administer exams, and grade essays and presentations. Adult and vocational education teachers also meet with students individually to discuss class progress and grades. Some courses are conducted as part of a long-distance education program (traditionally known as correspondence courses). For a distance education course, teachers prepare course materials, assignments, and work schedules to be sent to students, and then grade the work when it is turned in by the students.

REQUIREMENTS

High School
As an adult education teacher, you will likely focus on a particular area of study, so take the high school courses that best suit your interests. You'll also need to follow a college preparatory plan, taking courses in English, math, foreign language, history, and government. Speech and communications courses will help you prepare for speaking in front of groups of people. Writing skills are very important, no matter what subject you teach, because you'll be preparing reports, lesson plans, and grading essays.

Postsecondary Training
Before becoming an adult education teacher, you'll need to gain some professional experience in your area of teaching. A bachelor's degree is also usually required. Requirements vary according to the subject and level being taught, the organization or institution offering the course, and the state in which the instruction takes place. Specific skills, however, are often enough to secure a continuing education teaching position. For example, a person accomplished as a painter, with some professional success in the area, may be able to teach a course on painting even without a college degree or teaching certificate.

Certification or Licensing

There is no national certifying board for adult education teachers, but some states require their own teaching certification. Most community and junior colleges, however, require only a bachelor's degree of their teachers. Teachers in vocational education programs may have to be certified in their profession. If teaching English as a second language (ESL), you'll probably have to take some required workshops and seminars. For information on certification, contact local adult education programs and the department of education in the state in which you are interested in teaching.

Other Requirements

As a teacher, you should be able to deal with students at different skill levels, including some who might not have learned proper study habits or who have a different first language. This requires patience, as well as the ability to track the progress of each individual student. Good communication skills are essential, as you'll need to explain things clearly and to answer questions completely.

EXPLORING

Adult education classes are often held at high schools; if this is the case at your school, take the opportunity to discuss career questions with teachers before or after a class. You may also get the opportunity to observe one of these classes. Some of your high school teachers may teach adult or vocational education courses in the evenings; talk to them about the difference between teaching high school and teaching in an adult education program. Registering for a continuing education or vocational education course is another way of discovering the skills and disciplines needed to succeed in this field; if you have an interest in a particular subject not taught at your school, seek out classes at community colleges.

Your school may have a peer-tutoring program that would introduce you to the requirements of teaching. You could also volunteer to assist in special educational activities at a nursing home, church, synagogue, mosque, or community center.

EMPLOYERS

There are approximately 261,000 adult literacy, remedial, and self-enrichment teachers employed in the United States. More than one in five of these teachers is self-employed. Adult education teachers can find work in a variety of different schools and education programs. Community and junior colleges regularly have openings for teachers. Specially trained teachers can work for state-funded programs, such as literacy and ESL programs. Teachers are also hired for long-distance education programs and to lead continuing education courses for corporations and professional associations. Teachers are often needed in such institutions as prisons, hospitals, retirement communities, and group homes for disabled adults.

STARTING OUT

Most people entering this field have some professional experience in a particular area, a desire to share that knowledge with other adults, and a teaching certificate or academic degree. When pursuing work as an adult education teacher, you should contact colleges, private trade schools, vocational high schools, or other appropriate institutions to receive additional information about employment opportunities. Many colleges, technical schools, and state departments of education offer job lines or bulletin boards of job listings. You can also often find job openings in the classifieds of local newspapers.

ADVANCEMENT

A skilled adult or vocational education teacher may become a full-time teacher, school administrator, or director of a vocational guidance program. To be an administrator, a master's degree or a doctorate may be required. Advancement also may take the form of higher pay and additional teaching assignments.

EARNINGS

Earnings vary widely according to the subject, the number of courses taught, the teacher's experience, and the geographic region where the institution is located. According to the U.S. Department of Labor, adult literacy and remedial education teachers earned an average salary of $43,910 in 2006. The lowest paid 10 percent of these workers made less than $24,610, while the highest paid 10 percent earned $75,680 or more.

Many adult and vocational education teachers are employed part-time. They are often paid by the hour or by the course, with no health insurance or other benefits. Rates range from $6 to $50.

WORK ENVIRONMENT

Working conditions vary according to the type of class being taught and the number of students participating. Courses are usually taught in a classroom setting but may also be in a technical shop, laboratory, art studio, music room, or other location depending on the subject matter. Of course, when teaching in such settings as prisons or hospitals, adult education teachers must travel to the students as opposed to the students traveling to the teacher's classroom. Average class size is usually between 10 and 30 students but may vary, ranging from one-on-one instruction to large lectures attended by 60 or more students.

Some adult and vocational education teachers may only work nine or 10 months a year, with summers off. About half of the adult and vocational education teachers work part time, averaging anywhere from two to 20 hours of work per week. For those employed full time, the average workweek is between 35 and 40 hours. Much of the work is in the evening or on weekends.

OUTLOOK

Employment opportunities in the field of adult education are expected to grow much faster than the average for all occupations through 2016, according to the U.S. Department of Labor. Adults recognize the importance of further education and training for success in today's workplace. In fact, many courses are subsidized by companies that want their employees to be skilled in the latest trends and technology. According to the U.S. Department of Labor, the biggest growth areas are projected to be in computer- and Internet-related subjects, culinary arts, personal finance, arts and crafts, and self inprovement. As demand for adult and vocational education teachers continues to grow, major employers will be vocational high schools, private trade schools, community colleges, and private adult education enterprises.

Many "school-to-work" programs have evolved across the country as a result of the School-to-Work Opportunities Act of 1994. To prepare more graduating seniors for the high-wage jobs, "tech prep" programs offer course work in both academic and vocational subject matter. As more of these programs are developed, vocational education teachers will find many more opportunities to work in high schools and training schools.

FOR MORE INFORMATION

For information about conferences and publications, contact
American Association for Adult and Continuing Education
10111 Martin Luther King Jr. Highway, Suite 200C
Bowie, MD 20720-4200

Tel: 301-459-6261
Email: aaace10@aol.com
http://www.aaace.org

For information about publications, current legislation, and school-to-work programs, contact
Association for Career and Technical Education
1410 King Street
Alexandria, VA 22314-2749
Tel: 800-826-9972
Email: acte@acteonline.org
http://www.acteonline.org

For information about government programs, contact
U.S. Department of Education
400 Maryland Avenue, SW
Washington, DC 20202-0498
Tel: 800-872-5327
http://www.ed.gov

Career and Employment Counselors and Technicians

OVERVIEW

Career and employment counselors, who are also known as *vocational counselors,* provide advice to individuals or groups about occupations, careers, career decision making, career planning, and other career development-related questions or conflicts. *Career guidance technicians* collect pertinent information to support both the counselor and applicant during the job search. Approximately 260,000 educational, vocational, and school counselors are employed in the United States.

HISTORY

The first funded employment office in the United States was established in San Francisco in 1886. However, it was not until the turn of the century that public interest in improving educational conditions began to develop. The Civic Service House in Boston began the United States' first program of vocational guidance, and the Vocational Bureau was established in 1908 to help young people choose, train, and enter appropriate careers.

The idea of vocational counseling became so popular that by 1910 a national conference on vocational guidance was held in Boston. The federal government gave support to vocational

QUICK FACTS

School Subjects
Business
Psychology
Sociology

Personal Skills
Communication/ideas
Helping/teaching

Work Environment
Primarily indoors
Primarily one location

Minimum Education Level
Master's degree (counselors)
Some postsecondary training
(technicians)

Salary Range
$20,000 to $47,530 to
$100,000+ (counselors)
$20,000 to $30,000 to
$40,000 (technicians)

Certification or Licensing
Required by certain states
(counselors)
None available (technicians)

Outlook
About as fast as the average

DOT
166, 249 (counselors)
249 (technicians)

GOE
12.03.01

(continues)

QUICK FACTS

(continued)

NOC
4143, 4213 (counselors)
N/A (technicians)

O*NET-SOC
13-1071.00, 13-1071.01,
21-1012.00 (counselors)
N/A (technicians)

counseling by initiating a program to assist veterans of World War I in readjusting to civilian life. Agencies such as the Civilian Conservation Corps and the National Youth Administration provided vocational counseling during the Depression years.

On June 6, 1933, the Wagner-Peyser Act established the United States Employment Service. States came into the service one by one, with each state developing its own plan under the prescribed limits of the Act. By the end of World War II, the Veterans Administration was counseling more than 50,000 veterans each month. Other state and federal government agencies now involved with vocational guidance services include the Bureau of Indian Affairs, the Bureau of Apprenticeship and Training, and the Department of Education. In 1980, the National Career Development Association (NCDA), founded in 1913, established a committee for the pre-service and in-service training of vocational guidance personnel. The NCDA established a national credentialing process in 1984.

The profession of employment counseling has become important to the welfare of society as well as to the individuals within it. Each year millions of people need help in acquiring the kinds of information that make it possible for them to take advantage of today's career opportunities.

THE JOB

Certified career counselors help people to make decisions and to plan life and career directions. They tailor strategies and techniques to the specific needs of the person seeking help. Counselors conduct individual and group counseling sessions to help identify life and career goals. They administer and interpret tests and inventories to assess abilities and interests and identify career options. They may use career planning and occupational information to help individuals better understand the work world. They assist in developing individualized career plans, teach job-hunting strategies and skills, and help develop resumes. Sometimes this involves resolving personal conflicts on the job. They also provide support for people experiencing job stress, job loss, and career transition.

Vocational-rehabilitation counselors work with disabled individuals to help the counselees understand what skills they have to offer to an employer. A good counselor knows the working world and how to obtain detailed information about specific jobs. To assist with career decisions, counselors must know about the availability of jobs, the probable future of certain jobs, the education or training necessary to enter them, the kinds of salary or other benefits that certain jobs offer, the conditions that certain jobs impose on employees (night work, travel, work outdoors), and the satisfaction that certain jobs provide their employees. Professional career counselors work in both private and public settings and are certified by the National Board for Certified Counselors (NBCC).

College career planning counselors and *college placement counselors* work exclusively with the students of their universities or colleges. They may specialize in some specific area appropriate to the students and graduates of the school, such as law and education, as well as in part-time and summer work, internships, and field placements. In a liberal arts college, the students may need more assistance in identifying an appropriate career. To provide this assistance, the counselor administers interest and aptitude tests and interviews students to determine their career goals.

The counselor may work with currently enrolled students who are seeking internships and other work programs while still at school. Alumni who wish to make a career change also seek the services of the career counseling and placement office at their former schools.

College placement counselors also gather complete job information from prospective employers and make the information available to interested students and alumni. Just as counselors try to find applicants for particular job listings, they also must seek out jobs for specific applicants. To do this, they will call potential employers to encourage them to consider a qualified individual.

College and career planning and placement counselors are responsible for the arrangements and details of on-campus interviews by large corporations. They also maintain an up-to-date library of vocational guidance material and recruitment literature.

Counselors also give assistance in preparing the actual job search by helping the applicant to write resumes and letters of application, as well as by practicing interview skills through role-playing and other techniques. They also provide information on business procedures and personnel requirements in the applicant's chosen field. University-based counselors will set up online accounts on career Web sites for students, giving them access to information regarding potential employers.

Some career planning and placement counselors work with secondary school authorities, advising them on the needs of local industries and specific preparation requirements for both employment and further education. In two-year colleges the counselor may participate in the planning of course content, and in some smaller schools the counselor may be required to teach as well.

The principal duty of *career guidance technicians* is to help order, catalog, and file materials relating to job opportunities, careers, technical schools, scholarships, careers in the armed forces, and other programs. Guidance technicians also help students and teachers find materials relating to a student's interests and aptitudes. These various materials may be in the form of books, pamphlets, magazine articles, microfiche, videos, computer software, or other media.

Often, career guidance technicians help students take and score self-administered tests that determine their aptitude and interest in different careers or job-related activities. If the career guidance center has audiovisual equipment, such as VCRs, DVD players, or film or slide projectors, career guidance technicians are usually responsible for the equipment.

REQUIREMENTS

High School
In order to work in the career and employment counseling field, you must have at least a high school diploma. For most jobs in the field, however, higher education is required. In high school, in addition to studying a core curriculum, with courses in English, history, mathematics, and biology, you should take courses in psychology and sociology. You will also find it helpful to take business and computer science classes.

Postsecondary Training
In some states, the minimum educational requirement in career and vocational counseling is a graduate degree in counseling or a related field from a regionally accredited higher education institution, and a completed supervised counseling experience, which includes career counseling. A growing number of institutions offer post-master's degrees with training in career development and career counseling. Such programs are highly recommended if you wish to specialize in vocational and career counseling. These programs are frequently called advanced graduate specialist programs or certificates of advanced study programs.

For a career as a college career planning and placement counselor, the minimum educational requirement is commonly a master's degree in guidance and counseling, education, college student personnel work, behavioral science, or a related field. Graduate work includes courses in vocational and aptitude testing, counseling techniques, personnel management and occupational research, industrial relations, and group dynamics and organizational behavior.

As in any profession, there is usually an initial period of training for newly hired counselors and counselor trainees. Some of the skills you will need as an employment counselor, such as testing-procedures skills and interviewing skills, can be acquired only through on-the-job training.

When hiring a career guidance technician, most employers look for applicants who have completed two years of training beyond high school, usually at a junior, community, or technical college. These two-year programs, which usually lead to an associate's degree, may combine classroom instruction with practical or sometimes even on-the-job experience.

Certification or Licensing

The NBCC offers the national certified counselor (NCC) designation as well as the national certified school counselor (NCSC) designation. In order to apply for the NCC, you must have earned a master's degree with a major study in counseling and you must pass the National Counselor Examination. NCCs are certified for a period of five years. In order to be recertified, they must complete 100 contact clock hours of continuing education or pass the examination again. In order to receive the NCSC credential, you must complete the above requirements, plus gain field experience in school counseling as a graduate student and then complete three years of post-graduate supervised school counseling. Many states require some type of credentialing or certification for counselors, and all states require those who work in school settings to be certified.

Other Requirements

In order to succeed as a career counselor, you must have a good background in education, training, employment trends, the current labor market, and career resources. You should be able to provide your clients with information about job tasks, functions, salaries, requirements, and the future outlook of broad occupational fields.

Knowledge of testing techniques and measures of aptitude, achievement, interests, values, and personality is required. The ability to evaluate job performance and individual effectiveness is helpful. You must also have management and administrative skills.

Books to Read

Amundson, Norman, JoAnn Harris-Bowlsbey, and Spencer G. Niles. *Essential Elements of Career Counseling: Processes and Techniques.* 2d ed. Upper Saddle River, N.J.: Prentice Hall, 2008.

Bolles, Richard Nelson and Howard E. Figler. *The Career Counselor's Handbook.* 2d ed. Berkeley, Calif.: Ten Speed Press, 2007.

Brown, Duane. *Career Information, Career Counseling, and Career Development.* 9th ed. Boston: Allyn & Bacon, 2006.

Niles, Spencer G., Jane Goodman, and Mark Pope (eds.). *The Career Counseling Casebook: A Resource for Practitioners, Students, and Counselor Educators.* Broken Arrow, Okla.: National Career Development Association, 2001.

Pope, Mark, and Carole W. Minor (eds.). *Experiential Activities For Teaching Career Counseling Classes & Facilitating Career Groups.* Broken Arrow, Okla.: National Career Development Association, 2005.

Zunker, Vernon G. *Career Counseling: A Holistic Approach.* 7th ed. Belmont, Calif.: Wadsworth Publishing, 2006.

EXPLORING

Summer work in an employment agency is a good way to explore the field of employment counseling. Interviewing the director of a public or private agency may give you a better understanding of what the work involves and the qualifications such an organization requires of its counselors.

If you enjoy working with others, you will find helpful experiences working in the dean's or counselor's office. Many schools offer opportunities in peer tutoring, both in academics and in career guidance-related duties. (If your school does not have such a program in place, consider putting together a proposal to institute one. Your guidance counselor should be able to help you with this.) Your own experience in seeking summer jobs or part-time work is also valuable in learning what job seekers must confront in business or industry. You could write a feature story for your school newspaper on your and others' experiences in the working world.

If you are interested in becoming a career counselor, you should seek out professional career counselors and discuss the field with them. Most people are happy to talk about what they do.

While in high school, consider working part time or as a volunteer in a library. Such work can provide you with some of the basic skills for learning about information resources, cataloging, and filing. In addition, assisting schools or clubs with any media presentations, such as video or slide shows, will help you become familiar with the equipment used by counselors. You may also find it helpful to read publications relating to this field, such as *The National Certified Counselor* newsletter (http://www.nbcc.org/users/productseekers.htm).

EMPLOYERS

There are approximately 260,000 educational, vocational, and school counselors employed in the United States. Career and employment counselors work in guidance offices of high schools, colleges, and universities. They are also employed by state, federal, and other bureaus of employment, and by social service agencies.

STARTING OUT

Journals specializing in information for career counselors frequently have job listings or information on job hotlines and services. School career services offices also are good sources of information, both because of their standard practice of listing job openings from participating firms and because schools are a likely source of jobs for you as a career counselor. Placement officers will be aware of which schools are looking for applicants.

To enter the field of college career planning and placement, you might consider working for your alma mater as an assistant in the college or university career services office. Other occupational areas that provide an excellent background for college placement work include teaching, business, public relations, previous placement training, positions in employment agencies, and experience in psychological counseling.

Career guidance technicians should receive some form of career placement from schools offering training in that area. Newspapers may list entry-level jobs. One of the best methods, however, is to contact libraries and education centers directly to inquire about their needs for assistance in developing or staffing their career guidance centers.

ADVANCEMENT

Employment counselors in federal or state employment services or in other vocational counseling agencies are usually considered trainees for the first six months of their employment. During this time, they learn the specific skills that will be expected of them during their careers with these agencies. The first year of a new counselor's employment is probationary.

Positions of further responsibility include supervisory or administrative work, which may be attained by counselors after several years of experience on the job. Advancement to administrative positions often means giving up actual counseling work, which is not an advantage to those who enjoy working with people in need of counseling.

Opportunities for advancement for college counselors—to assistant and associate placement director, director of student personnel services, or similar administrative positions—depend largely on the type of college or university and the size of the staff. In general, a doctorate is preferred and may be necessary for advancement.

With additional education, career guidance technicians can advance to become career and employment counselors.

EARNINGS

Salaries vary greatly within the career and vocational counseling field. The U.S. Department of Labor (USDL) places career counselors within the category of educational, vocational, and school counselors. The median yearly earnings for this group were $47,530 in 2006, according to the USDL. The lowest paid 10 percent of these workers earned $27,240 or less per year, and the highest paid 10 percent made $75,920 or more annually. The department further broke down salaries by type of employer: Those working for elementary and secondary schools had mean annual incomes of $55,560 in 2006; for junior colleges, $53,650; for colleges and universities, $44,730; for individual and family services, $35,020; and for vocational rehabilitation services, $34,320. Annual earnings of career counselors vary greatly among educational institutions, with larger institutions offering the highest salaries. Counselors in business or industry tend to earn higher salaries.

In private practice, the salary range is even wider. Some practitioners earn as little as $20,000 per year, and others, such as elite "headhunters" who recruit corporate executives and other high-salaried positions, earn in excess of $100,000 per year.

Salaries for career guidance technicians vary according to education and experience and the geographic location of the job. In general, career guidance technicians who are graduates of two-year post high school training programs can expect to receive starting salaries averaging $20,000 to $25,000 a year.

Benefits depend on the employer, but they usually include paid holidays and vacation time, retirement plans, and, for those at some educational institutions, reduced tuition.

WORK ENVIRONMENT

Employment counselors usually work about 40 hours a week, but some agencies are more flexible. Counseling is done in offices designed to be free from noise and distractions, to allow confidential discussions with clients.

College career planning and placement counselors also normally work a 40-hour week, although irregular hours and overtime are frequently required during the peak recruiting period. They generally work on a 12-month basis.

Career guidance technicians work in very pleasant surroundings, usually in the career guidance office of a college or vocational school. They will interact with a great number of students, some of whom are eagerly looking for work, and others who are more tense and anxious. The technician must remain unruffled in order to ease any tension and provide a quiet atmosphere.

OUTLOOK

Employment in the field of employment counseling is expected to grow about as fast as the average for all occupations through 2016, according to the U.S. Department of Labor. One reason for this steady growth is increased school enrollments, even at the college level, which means more students needing the services of career counselors. Another reason is that there are more counselor jobs than graduates of counseling programs. Opportunities should also be available in government agencies as many states institute welfare-to-work programs or simply cut welfare benefits. And finally, in this age of outsourcing and lack of employment security, "downsized" workers, those re-entering the workforce, and those looking for second careers all create a need for the skills of career and employment counselors.

FOR MORE INFORMATION

For a variety of career resources for career seekers and career counseling professionals, contact the following organizations:

American Counseling Association
5999 Stevenson Avenue
Alexandria, VA 22304-3300

Tel: 800-347-6647
http://www.counseling.org

Career Planning & Adult Development Network
543 Vista Mar Avenue
Pacifica, CA 94044-1951
Tel: 650-359-6911
Email: admin@careernetwork.org
http://www.careernetwork.org

For resume and interview tips, general career information, and advice from experts, contact or visit the following Web site:
National Association of Colleges and Employers (NACE)
62 Highland Avenue
Bethlehem, PA 18017-9085
Tel: 800-544-5272
http://www.naceweb.org

For information on certification, contact
National Board for Certified Counselors
3 Terrace Way
Greensboro, NC 27403-3660
Tel: 336-547-0607
Email: nbcc@nbcc.org
http://www.nbcc.org

For more information on career counselors, contact
National Career Development Association
305 North Beech Circle
Broken Arrow, OK 74012-2293
Tel: 918-663-7060
http://ncda.org

INTERVIEW

Kim Dunisch is the director of career services at Concordia University Wisconsin in Mequon, Wisconsin. She discussed her career with the editors of Careers in Focus: Education.

Q. Please tell us a little about yourself and Concordia University Wisconsin?

A. I have been with Concordia University Wisconsin for almost two years now. For my first year I was in admissions in Adult

Education. I just came into the role as director of career services in September. I am also in the process of creating a class for our students who are undecided about their majors, which I will be teaching in the Fall of 2008.

Lutherans in Wisconsin founded Concordia College in 1881. In 1978, Concordia was authorized by the Missouri Synod to become a four-year accredited college. In a far-sighted move in 1982, the Missouri Synod purchased the former campus of the School Sisters of Notre Dame in Mequon, Wisconsin. The attractive campus consists of 192 acres on the shore of Lake Michigan, just 15 minutes north of downtown Milwaukee. On August 27, 1989, changing the college to university status was approved by the Board of Regents. Concordia University Wisconsin became the first university in the Missouri Synod college system. Concordia University Wisconsin is accredited by the Commission on Institutions of Higher Education of the North Central Association of Colleges and Schools. Today, Concordia has an undergraduate enrollment of more than 1,600 students from 48 states and more than 25 countries. Concordia offers more than 55 majors and 20 minors, on which the average class size is 17 students. Concordia is a NCAA III member of the Northern Athletics Conference. Our mission at Concordia University is to provide a Lutheran higher education community committed to helping students develop mind, body, and spirit for service to Christ in the church and in the world.

Q. Why did you decide to enter this field?
A. While I was in college, I really utilized my career service office. I would think about how that seemed like a "neat" job at the time, but it wasn't what I was going to school for. During college I was involved with a student organization called Delta Epsilon Chi, through which I now assist current students as an alumni. Many of these students have asked for my advice on resumes and cover letters and since I came from a management and hiring background, I felt equipped enough to assist them. Before entering this role I worked in admissions. I really enjoyed what I did there, but always thought about where else I would want to move to within the university if I ever made a move. Career Services was one of two departments in which I thought I would work well. The other was Student Life because I love to plan events, which I also get to do in Career Services—so it's a win-win situation.

Q. What do you like most and least about your job?

A. There are so many things that I like about my job. The thing that I like most about my job is assisting students and seeing them take my advice and succeed by getting the interview or the job. It's great to see that student who doesn't have a clue where to start with a resume come back after a few visits with me and have it perfected.

　　The thing that I like least about my job is that since I'm new, I have all these great ideas of how I envision the office and what types of services I would like to eventually offer, but I never seem to have the time to get to all of them due to all the hats I wear.

Q. What type of educational path did you pursue to enter this career?

A. I went to a technical college and earned three associate degrees—marketing, fashion marketing, and retail management. I then went on to a state university where I earned my bachelor's degree in retail management with a fashion marketing emphasis. After working for two years, I decided to pursue my MBA while I was still working full time. I have my MBA with a marketing emphasis. I think my background really helps me in this role because you really have to market and sell your services to the students and get them to attend events that you have planned. I'm always coming up with a new way to target students and ways to offer promotions to them as well. You also have to sell your university and students to employers to get them to assist you when needed.

Q. What are the most important professional qualities for people in your career?

A. You have to be a people person as far as assisting students and making those employer connections. You also have to be able to change your style to relate the same topic to different personalities; not all students will understand something in the same way. You will also want to continue your education on a professional development level to be able to assist your students with current information and resources. Another thing you will need to utilize is your time management skills as well as your monetary budget skills. And last, but not least, you really need to enjoy helping people.

College Administrators

OVERVIEW

College administrators coordinate and oversee programs such as admissions and financial aid in public and private colleges and universities. They frequently work with teams of people to develop and manage student services. Administrators also oversee specific academic divisions of colleges and universities. Approximately 131,000 college administrators are employed in the United States.

HISTORY

Before the Civil War, most U.S. colleges and universities managed their administration with a president, a treasurer, and a part-time librarian. Members of the faculty often were responsible for the administrative tasks of the day, and there was no uniformity in college admissions requirements.

By 1860, the average number of administrative officers in U.S. colleges was still only four. However, as the job of running an institution expanded in scope in response to ever-increasing student enrollment, the responsibilities of administration began to splinter. After creating positions for registrar, secretary of faculty, chief business officer, and a number of departmental deans, most schools next hired a director of admissions to oversee the application and acceptance of students. In addition, several prominent college presidents, Charles Eliot of Harvard and Nicholas Butler of Columbia among them, saw the need to establish organizations whose purpose would be to put an end to the chaos. The College Entrance Examination Board was formed to create standardized college entrance requirements. By 1910, there

QUICK FACTS

School Subjects
Business
English
Speech

Personal Skills
Helping/teaching
Leadership/management

Work Environment
Primarily indoors
Primarily one location

Minimum Education Level
Bachelor's degree

Salary Range
$41,120 to $73,990 to
$360,000+

Certification or Licensing
None available

Outlook
Faster than the average

DOT
090

GOE
12.01.01

NOC
0312

O*NET-SOC
11-9033.00

were 25 leading colleges using the Board's exams. Today, most colleges require that a student submit standardized test scores, such as the SAT or ACT, when applying.

After World War II, returning veterans entered America's colleges and universities by the thousands. With this great influx of students, college administrators were needed to improve the organization of the university system. During this time, financial aid administration also became a major program. Today, as the costs of a college education continue to rise dramatically, college financial aid administrators are needed to help students and parents find loans, grants, scholarships, and work-study programs.

THE JOB

A college administrator's work is demanding and diverse. An administrator is responsible for a wide range of tasks in areas such as counseling services, admissions, alumni affairs, financial aid, academics, and business. The following are some of the different types of college administrators, but keep in mind that this is only a partial list. It takes many administrators in many different departments to run a college.

Many college and university administrators are known as *deans*. Deans are the administrative heads of specific divisions or groups within the university, and are in charge of overseeing the activities and policies of that division. One type of dean is an *academic dean*. Academic deans are concerned with such issues as the requirements for a major, the courses offered, and the faculty hired within a specific academic department or division. The field of academic dean includes such titles as dean of the college of humanities, dean of social and behavioral sciences, and dean of the graduate school, just to name a few. The *dean of students* is responsible for the student-affairs program, often including such areas as student housing, organizations, clubs, and activities.

Registrars prepare class schedules and final exam schedules. They maintain computer records of student data, such as grades and degree requirements. They prepare school catalogs and student handbooks. *Associate registrars* assist in running the school registrar's office.

Recruiters visit high school campuses and college fairs to provide information about their school and to interest students in applying for admission. They develop relationships with high school administrators and arrange to meet with counselors, students, and parents.

Financial aid administrators direct the scholarship, grant, and loan programs that provide financial assistance to students and help them meet the costs of tuition, fees, books, and other living expenses.

The administrator keeps students informed of the financial assistance available to them and helps answer student and parent questions and concerns. At smaller colleges, this work might be done by a single person, the *financial aid officer.* At larger colleges and universities, the staff might be bigger, and the financial aid officer will head a department and direct the activities of *financial aid counselors,* who handle most of the personal contact with students.

Other college administrators include *college admissions counselors*, who review records, interview prospective students, and process applications for admission. *Alumni directors* oversee the alumni associations of colleges and universities. An alumni director maintains relationships with the graduates of the college primarily for fund-raising purposes.

Such jobs as university *president, vice president,* and *provost* are among the highest-ranking college and university administrative positions. Generally the president and vice president act as high-level managers, overseeing the rest of a college's administration. They handle business concerns, press relations, public image, and community involvement, and they listen to faculty and administration concerns, often casting the final vote on issues such as compensation, advancement, and tenure. At most schools, the provost is in charge of the many collegiate deans. Working through the authority of the deans, the provost manages the college faculty. The provost also oversees budgets, the academic schedule, event planning, and participates in faculty hiring and promotion decisions.

REQUIREMENTS
High School
A well-rounded education is important for anyone pursuing top administrative positions. To prepare for a job in college administration, take accounting and math courses, as you may be dealing with financial records and student statistics. To be a dean of a college, you must have good communication skills, so you should take courses in English literature and composition. Also, speech courses are important, as you'll be required to give presentations and represent your department at meetings and conferences. Follow your guidance counselor's college preparatory plan, which will likely include courses in science, foreign language, history, and sociology.

Postsecondary Training
Education requirements for jobs in college administration depend on the size of the school and the job position. Some assistant positions may not require anything more than a few years of experience in

an office. For most jobs in college administration, however, you'll need at least a bachelor's degree. For the top administrative positions, you'll need a master's or a doctorate. A bachelor's degree in any field is usually acceptable for pursuing this career. After you've received your bachelor's, you may choose to pursue a master's in student personnel, administration, or subjects such as economics, psychology, and sociology. Other important studies include education, counseling, information processing, business, and finance. In order to become a college dean, you'll need a doctoral degree and many years of experience with a college or university. Your degree may be in your area of study or in college administration.

Other Requirements

As a college administrator, you should be very organized and able to manage a busy office of assistants. Some offices require more organization than others; for example, a financial aid office handles the records and aid disbursement for the entire student body and requires a director with an eye for efficiency and the ability to keep track of the various sources of student funding. As a dean, however, you'll work in a smaller office, concentrating more on issues concerning faculty and committees, and you'll rely on your diplomatic skills for maintaining an efficient and successful department. People skills are valuable for college deans, as you'll be representing your department both within the university and at national conferences.

Whatever the administrative position, it is important to have patience and tact to handle a wide range of personalities as well as an emotional steadiness when confronted with unusual and unexpected situations.

EXPLORING

To learn something about what the job of an administrator entails, talk to your high school principal and superintendent. Also, interview administrators at colleges and universities. Many of their office phone numbers are listed in college directories. The email addresses of the administrators of many different departments, from deans to registrars, are often published on college Web sites. You should also discuss the career with the college recruiters who visit your high school. Also, familiarize yourself with all the various aspects of running a college and university by looking at college student handbooks and course catalogs. Most handbooks list all the offices and administrators and how they assist students and faculty.

EMPLOYERS

Approximately 131,000 college administrators are employed in the United States. Administrators are needed all across the country to run colleges and universities. Job opportunities exist at public and private institutions, community colleges, and universities both large and small. In a smaller college, an administrator may run more than one department. There are more job openings for administrators in universities serving large student bodies.

STARTING OUT

There are several different types of entry-level positions available in the typical college administrative office. If you can gain part-time work or an internship in admissions or another office while you are still in school, you will have a great advantage when seeking work in this field after graduation. Any other experience in an administrative or managerial position that involves working with people or with computerized data is also helpful. Entry-level positions often involve filing, data processing, and updating records or charts. You might also move into a position as an administrator after working as a college professor. Deans in colleges and universities have usually worked many years as tenured professors.

The department of human resources in most colleges and universities maintains a listing of job openings at the institution and will often advertise the positions nationally. The *Chronicle of Higher Education* (http://www.chronicle.com) is a newspaper with national job listings. The College and University Professional Association for Human Resources (http://www.cupahr.org) also maintains a job list.

ADVANCEMENT

Entry-level positions, which usually require only a bachelor's degree, include admissions counselors, who advise students regarding admissions requirements and decisions, and *evaluators,* who check high school transcripts and college transfer records to determine whether applying students should be admitted. Administrative assistants are hired for the offices of registrars, financial aid departments, and deans.

Advancement from any of these positions will depend on the manner in which an office is organized as well as how large it is. One may move up to assistant director or associate director, or, in a larger office, into any specialized divisions such as minority admissions or financial aid counseling. Advancement also may come through transferring to other departments, schools, or systems.

Workshops and seminars are available through professional associations for those interested in staying informed and becoming more knowledgeable in the field, but it is highly unlikely that an office employee will gain the top administrative level without a graduate degree.

EARNINGS

Salaries for college administrators vary widely among two-year and four-year colleges and among public and private institutions, but they are generally comparable to those of college faculty. According to the U.S. Department of Labor, the median salary for education administrators was $73,990 in 2006. The lowest paid 10 percent of administrators earned $41,120 or less per year, while the highest paid made $137,900 or more annually.

The College and University Professional Association for Human Resources reports the following median annual salaries for college administrators by profession: academic deans, $68,774 (continuing education) to $362,508 (medicine); college president, $207,999; director, student health services (physician), $137,709; chief admissions officer, $75,920; director of student financial aid, $68,000; registrar, $66,008.

According to a study by the *Chronicle of Higher Education,* the average pay for private liberal arts college presidents was $243,541 in 2004. Public-university presidents earned median annual salaries of $360,000 in 2005. Though college presidents can earn high salaries, they are often not as high as earnings of other top administrators and even some college coaches. For example, competition can drive up the pay for highly desired medical specialists, economics educators, or football coaches.

Most colleges and universities provide excellent benefits packages including health insurance, paid vacation, sick leave, and tuition remission. Higher-level administrators such as presidents, deans, and provosts often receive bonuses such as access to special university privileges.

WORK ENVIRONMENT

College and universities are usually pleasant places to be employed. Offices are often spacious and comfortable, and the campus may be a scenic, relaxing work setting.

Employment in most administrative positions is usually on a 12-month basis. Many of the positions, such as admissions director, financial aid counselor, and dean of students, require a great deal of direct contact with students, and so working hours may vary according to student needs. It is not unusual for college administrators to work long hours during peak enrollment periods, such as the beginning of each quarter or semester. During these periods, the office can be fast paced and stressful as administrators work to assist as many students as possible. Directors are sometimes required to work evenings and weekends to provide broader student access to administrative services. In addition, administrators are sometimes required to travel to other colleges, career fairs, high schools, and professional conferences.

OUTLOOK

The U.S. Department of Labor predicts that employment for education administrators at the postsecondary level will grow faster than the average for all occupations through 2016. Competition for these prestigious positions, however, will be stiff. Many faculty at institutions of higher learning have the educational and experience requirements for these jobs. Candidates may face less competition for positions in nonacademic areas, such as admissions or fund-raising. Those who are already working within a department will have the best chances of getting administrative positions. Opportunities should be best for administrators employed by private and for-profit colleges and universities.

FOR MORE INFORMATION

For information on publications and membership, contact
**American Association of Collegiate Registrars and
    Admissions Officers**
One Dupont Circle, NW, Suite 520
Washington, DC 20036-1171
Tel: 202-293-9161
http://www.aacrao.org

For information about publications, current legislation, and membership, contact the following organizations:
American Association of University Administrators
PO Box 630101
Little Neck, NY 11363-0101
Tel: 347-235-4822
http://www.aaua.org

Association of College Administration Professionals
PO Box 1389
Staunton, VA 24402-1389
Tel: 540-885-1873
Email: acap@cfw.com
http://www.acap.org

For job listings and information about membership, contact
College and University Professional Association for Human Resources
1811 Commons Point Drive
Knoxville, TN 37932-1989
Tel: 865-637-7673
http://www.cupahr.org

National Association of College and University Business Officers
1110 Vermont Avenue, NW, Suite 800
Washington, DC 20005-3593
Tel: 800-462-4916
http://www.nacubo.org

For information on undergraduate fellowships, contact
National Association of Student Personnel Administrators
1875 Connecticut Avenue, NW, Suite 418
Washington, DC 20009-5737
Tel: 202-265-7500
http://www.naspa.org

College Professors

OVERVIEW

College professors instruct undergraduate and graduate students in specific subjects at colleges and universities. They are responsible for lecturing classes, leading small seminar groups, and creating and grading examinations. They also may conduct research, write for publication, and aid in college administration. Approximately 1.7 million postsecondary teachers are employed in the United States.

HISTORY

The concept of colleges and universities goes back many centuries. These institutions evolved slowly from monastery schools, which trained a select few for certain professions, notably theology. Outside of academia, the terms *college* and *university* have become virtually interchangeable in America, although originally they designated two very different kinds of institutions.

Two of the most notable early European universities were the University of Bologna in Italy, thought to have been established in the 12th century, and the University of Paris, which was chartered in 1201. These universities were considered to be the models after which other European universities were patterned. Oxford University in England was probably established during the 12th century. Oxford served as a model for early American colleges and universities and today is still considered one of the world's leading institutions.

Harvard, the first U.S. college, was established in 1636. Its stated purpose

QUICK FACTS

School Subjects
English
History
Speech

Personal Skills
Communication/ideas
Helping/teaching

Work Environment
Primarily indoors
Primarily one location

Minimum Education Level
Master's degree

Salary Range
$42,609 to $73,207 to
$98,974+

Certification or Licensing
None available

Outlook
Much faster than the average

DOT
090

GOE
12.03.02

NOC
4121

O*NET-SOC
25-1011.00, 25-1021.00,
25-1022.00, 25.1031.00,
25-1032.00, 25-1041.00,
25-1043.00, 25-1051.00,
25-1054.00, 25-1061.00,
25-1066.00, 25-1067.00,
25-1071.00, 25-1072.00,
25-1081.00, 25-1082.00,
25-1111.00–25-1113.00,
25-1121.00–25-1126.00,
25-1191.00–25-1194.00

was to train men for the ministry; the early colleges were all established for religious training. With the growth of state-supported institutions in the early 18th century, the process of freeing the curriculum from ties with the church began. The University of Virginia established the first liberal arts curriculum in 1825, and these innovations were later adopted by many other colleges and universities.

Although the original colleges in the United States were patterned after Oxford University, they later came under the influence of German universities. During the 19th century, more than 9,000 Americans went to Germany to study. The emphasis in German universities was on the scientific method. Most of the people who had studied in Germany returned to the United States to teach in universities, bringing this objective, factual approach to education and to other fields of learning.

In 1833, Oberlin College in Oberlin, Ohio, became the first college founded as a coeducational institution. In 1836, the first women-only college, Wesleyan Female College, was founded in Macon, Georgia.

The junior college movement in the United States has been one of the most rapidly growing educational developments. Junior colleges first came into being just after the turn of the 20th century.

THE JOB

College and university faculty members teach at junior colleges or at four-year colleges and universities. At four-year institutions, most faculty members are *assistant professors, associate professors,* or *full professors.* These three types of professorships differ in status, job responsibilities, and salary. Assistant professors are new faculty members who are working to get tenure (status as a permanent professor); they seek to advance to associate and then to full professorships.

College professors perform three main functions: teaching, advising, and research. Their most important responsibility is to teach students. Their role within a college department will determine the level of courses they teach and the number of courses per semester. Most professors work with students at all levels, from college freshmen to graduate students. They may head several classes a semester or only a few a year. Some of their classes will have large enrollment, while graduate seminars may consist of only 12 or fewer students. Though college professors may spend fewer than 10 hours a week in the actual classroom, they spend many hours preparing lectures and lesson plans, grading papers and exams, and preparing grade reports. They also schedule office hours during the week to be available to students outside of the lecture hall, and they meet with students individually throughout the semester. In the classroom, professors lecture, lead discussions, administer exams, and assign textbook readings and other research. In some courses, they rely heavily on laboratories to transmit course material.

Another important professorial responsibility is advising students. Not all faculty members serve as advisers, but those who do must set aside large blocks of time to guide students through the program. College professors who serve as advisers may have any number of students assigned to them, from fewer than 10 to more than 100, depending on the administrative policies of the college. Their responsibilities may involve looking over a planned program of studies to make sure the students meet requirements for graduation, or may involve working intensively with each student on many aspects of college life.

The third responsibility of college and university faculty members is research and publication. Faculty members who are heavily involved in research programs sometimes are assigned a smaller teaching load. College professors publish their research findings in various scholarly journals. They also write books based on their research or on their own knowledge and experience in the field. Most textbooks are written by college and university teachers. In arts-based programs, such as master's of fine arts programs in painting, writing, and theater, professors practice their craft and exhibit their art work in various ways. For example, a painter or photographer will have gallery showings, while a poet will publish in literary journals.

Publishing a significant amount of work has been the traditional standard by which assistant professors prove themselves worthy of becoming permanent, tenured faculty. Typically, pressure to publish is greatest for assistant professors. Pressure to publish increases again if an associate professor wishes to be considered for a promotion to full professorship.

In recent years, some liberal arts colleges have recognized that the pressure to publish is taking faculty away from their primary duties to students, and these institutions have begun to place a decreasing emphasis on publishing and more on performance in the classroom. Professors in junior colleges face less pressure to publish than those in four-year institutions.

Some faculty members eventually rise to the position of *department chair,* where they govern the affairs of an entire department,

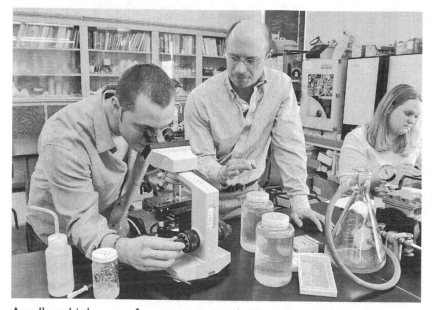

A college biology professor supervises his students as they examine germ specimens with a microscope. *(James Marshall, The Image Works)*

such as English, mathematics, or biological sciences. Department chairs, faculty, and other professional staff members are aided in their myriad duties by *graduate assistants,* who may help develop teaching materials, conduct research, give examinations, teach lower level courses, and carry out other activities.

Some college professors may also conduct classes in an extension program. In such a program, they teach evening and weekend courses for the benefit of people who would otherwise be unable to take advantage of the institution's resources. They may travel away from the campus and meet with a group of students at another location. They may work full time for the extension division or may divide their time between on-campus and off-campus teaching.

Distance learning programs, an increasingly popular option for students, allow professors to use today's technologies to remain in one place while teaching students who are at a variety of locations simultaneously. The professor's duties, like those when teaching correspondence courses conducted by mail, include grading work that students send in at periodic intervals and advising students of their progress. Computers, the Internet, email, and video conferencing are some of the technological tools that allow professors and students to communicate in "real time" in a virtual classroom setting. Meetings may be scheduled during the same time as traditional classes or during evenings and weekends. Professors who do this work are sometimes known as *extension work, correspondence,* or *distance learning instructors.* They may teach online courses in addition to other classes or may have distance learning as their primary teaching responsibility.

The *junior college instructor* has many of the same kinds of responsibilities as the teacher in a four-year college or university. Because junior colleges offer only a two-year program, they teach only undergraduates.

REQUIREMENTS

High School

Your high school's college preparatory program likely includes courses in English, science, foreign language, history, math, and government. In addition, you should take courses in speech to get a sense of what it will be like to lecture to a group of students. Your school's debate team can also help you develop public speaking skills, along with research skills.

Postsecondary Training

At least one advanced degree in your field of study is required to be a professor in a college or university. The master's degree is considered the minimum standard, and graduate work beyond the master's is usually desirable. If you hope to advance in academic rank above instructor, most institutions require a doctorate.

In the last year of your undergraduate program, you'll apply to graduate programs in your area of study. Standards for admission to a graduate program can be high and the competition heavy, depending on the school. Once accepted into a program, your responsibilities will be similar to those of your professors—in addition to attending seminars, you'll research, prepare articles for publication, and teach some undergraduate courses.

You may find employment in a junior college with only a master's degree. Advancement in responsibility and in salary, however, is more likely to come if you have earned a doctorate.

Other Requirements

You should enjoy reading, writing, and researching. Not only will you spend many years studying in school, but your whole career will be based on communicating your thoughts and ideas. People skills are important because you'll be dealing directly with students, administrators, and other faculty members on a daily basis. You should feel comfortable in a role of authority and possess self-confidence.

EXPLORING

Your high school teachers use many of the same skills as college professors, so talk to your teachers about their careers and their college experiences. You can develop your own teaching experience by volunteering at a community center, working at a day care center, or working at a summer camp. Also, spend some time on a college campus to get a sense of the environment. Write to colleges for their admissions brochures and course catalogs (or check them out online); read about the faculty members and the courses they teach. Before visiting college campuses, make arrangements to speak to professors who teach courses that interest you. These professors may allow you to sit in on their classes and observe. Also, make appointments with college advisers and with people in the admissions and recruitment offices. If your grades are good enough, you might be able to serve as a teaching assistant during your undergraduate years, which can give you experience leading discussions and grading papers.

EMPLOYERS

Employment opportunities vary based on area of study and education. Most universities have many different departments that hire faculty. With a doctorate, a number of publications, and a record of good teaching, professors should find opportunities in universities all across the country. There are more than 3,800 colleges and universities in the United States. Professors teach in undergraduate and graduate programs. The teaching jobs at doctoral institutions are usually better paying and more prestigious. The most sought-after positions are those that offer tenure. Teachers that have only a master's degree will be limited to opportunities with junior colleges, community colleges, and some small private institutions. There are approximately 1.7 million postsecondary teachers employed in the United States.

STARTING OUT

You should start the process of finding a teaching position while you are in graduate school. The process includes developing a curriculum vitae (a detailed, academic resume), writing for publication, assisting with research, attending conferences, and gaining teaching

Facts About Community Colleges, 2007

- There are 1,195 community colleges in the United States.
- Approximately 11.6 million students are enrolled in community college.
- 60 percent of students attend school part time.
- The average age of students is 29.
- Women make up 59 percent of community college students.
- Minorities make up 34 percent of students at community colleges. Hispanic students make up 14 percent of minority students attending community colleges; African Americans, 13 percent; Asian/Pacific Islanders, 6 percent; and Native Americans, 1 percent.
- The average annual tuition at public community colleges is $2,272.
- The most popular community college programs: registered nursing, law enforcement, licensed practical nursing, radiology, and computer technologies.
- The average expected lifetime earnings of associate degree graduates are estimated at $1.6 million. This is $400,000 more than the expected earnings for those with only a high school diploma.

Source: American Association of Community Colleges

experience and recommendations. Many students begin applying for teaching positions while finishing their graduate program. For most positions at four-year institutions, you must travel to large conferences where interviews can be arranged with representatives from the universities to which you have applied.

Because of the competition for tenure-track positions, you may have to work for a few years in temporary positions, visiting various schools as an *adjunct professor*. Some professional associations maintain lists of teaching opportunities in their areas. They may also make lists of applicants available to college administrators looking to fill an available position.

ADVANCEMENT

The normal pattern of advancement is from instructor to assistant professor, to associate professor, to full professor. All four academic ranks are concerned primarily with teaching and research. College faculty members who have an interest in and a talent for administration may be advanced to chair of a department or to dean of their college. A few become college or university presidents or other types of administrators.

The instructor is usually an inexperienced college teacher. He or she may hold a doctorate or may have completed all the Ph.D. requirements except for the dissertation. Most colleges look upon the rank of instructor as the period during which the college is trying out the teacher. Instructors usually are advanced to the position of assistant professor within three to four years. Assistant professors are given up to about six years to prove themselves worthy of tenure, and if they do so, they become associate professors. Some professors choose to remain at the associate level. Others strive to become full professors and receive greater status, salary, and responsibilities.

Most colleges have clearly defined promotion policies from rank to rank for faculty members, and many have written statements about the number of years in which instructors and assistant professors may remain in grade. Administrators in many colleges hope to encourage younger faculty members to increase their skills and competencies and thus to qualify for the more responsible positions of associate professor and full professor.

EARNINGS

Earnings vary depending on the departments professors work in, the size of the school, the type of school (for example, public, private, or women's only), and by the level of position the professor holds. In its 2006-07 salary survey, the American Association of University Professors (AAUP) reported the average yearly income for all full-time faculty was $73,207. It also reports that professors earned the following average salaries by rank: full professors, $98,974; associate professors, $69,911; assistant professors, $58,662; instructors, $42,609; and lecturers, $48,289. Full professors working in disciplines such as law, architecture, business and related fields, health professions, computer and information sciences, and engineering have the highest salaries. Lower paying disciplines include theology, recreation and fitness studies, English, liberal arts/humanities, and visual and performing arts.

Many professors try to increase their earnings by completing research, publishing in their field, or teaching additional courses. Professors working on the west coast and the east coast of the United States and those working at doctorate-granting institutions tend to have the highest salaries.

Benefits for full-time faculty typically include health insurance and retirement funds and, in some cases, stipends for travel related to research, housing allowances, and tuition waivers for dependents.

WORK ENVIRONMENT

A college or university is usually a pleasant place in which to work. Campuses bustle with all types of activities and events, stimulating ideas, and a young, energetic population. Much prestige comes with success as a professor and scholar; professors have the respect of students, colleagues, and others in their community.

Depending on the size of the department, college professors may have their own office, or they may have to share an office with one or more colleagues. Their department may provide them with a computer, Internet access, and research assistants. College professors are also able to do much of their office work at home. They can arrange their schedule around class hours, academic meetings, and the established office hours when they meet with students. Most college teachers work more than 40 hours each week. Although college professors may teach only two or three classes a semester, they spend many hours preparing for lectures, examining student work, and conducting research.

OUTLOOK

The U.S. Department of Labor predicts much-faster-than-average employment growth for college and university professors through 2016. College enrollment is projected to grow due to an increased number of 18- to 24-year-olds, an increased number of adults returning to college, and an increased number of foreign-born students. Additionally, opportunities for college teachers will be good in areas including the biological sciences, business, and nursing and other health fields. Retirement of current faculty members will also provide job openings. However, competition for full-time, tenure-track positions at four-year schools will remain very strong.

Opportunities should be very strong at community colleges and other academic institutions that provide career and technical education, as these types of institutions continue to expand their course offerings to satisfy industry demand.

A number of factors threaten to change the way colleges and universities hire faculty. Some university leaders are developing more business-based methods of running their schools, focusing on profits and budgets. This can affect college professors in a number of ways.

One of the biggest effects is in the replacement of tenure-track faculty positions with part-time instructors. These part-time instructors include adjunct faculty, visiting professors, and graduate students. Organizations such as the AAUP and the American Federation of Teachers are working to prevent the loss of these full-time jobs, as well as to help part-time instructors receive better pay and benefits. Other issues involve the development of long-distance education departments in many schools. Though these correspondence courses have become very popular in recent years, many professionals believe that students in long-distance education programs receive only a second-rate education. A related concern is about the proliferation of computers in the classroom. Some courses consist only of instruction by computer software and the Internet. The effects of these alternative methods on the teaching profession will be offset somewhat by the expected increases in college enrollment in coming years.

FOR MORE INFORMATION

To read about the issues affecting college professors, contact the following organizations:

American Association of University Professors
1012 14th Street, NW, Suite 500
Washington, DC 20005-3406
Tel: 202-737-5900
Email: aaup@aaup.org
http://www.aaup.org

American Federation of Teachers
555 New Jersey Avenue, NW
Washington, DC 20001-2029
Tel: 202-879-4400
Email: online@aft.org
http://www.aft.org

Computer Trainers

OVERVIEW

Computer trainers teach topics related to all aspects of using computers in the workplace, including personal computer (PC) software, operating systems for both stand-alone and networked systems, management tools for networks, and software applications for mainframe computers and specific industry management. Trainers work for training companies and software developers, either on the permanent staff or as independent consultants. They may produce training materials, including disk-based multimedia technology-delivered learning, instructor-led courseware, skills assessment, videos, and classroom teaching manuals.

HISTORY

The field of computer training began around 1983, when the computer industry exploded with the introduction of the first PCs. With all of the new software packages being released, individual information technology (IT) and information services (IS) departments could not possibly keep up with the amount of training their employees needed. Software vendor companies started sending their employees out to teach new purchasers how to use their products, and a new section of the computer industry was born.

In the beginning, computer training was conducted like any other training, in a classroom setting with an instructor. Although that type of training is still prevalent today, current training methods incorporate new technology. According to the American Society for Training and Development (ASTD), workplace educators are turning to technology to deliver their instructions. Developments in hardware, computer networking, multimedia software, and video conferencing have tremendous potential for multiple-site instruction and training closer to people's work sites.

Technological developments constantly change the processes by which work is done. As a result, computer trainers must be up to date on the latest developments and improvements in computer systems and programs. The ASTD also notes that training departments are finding new ways to deliver computer training, by using support networks of internal and external training providers, including consultants, community colleges, and universities.

THE JOB

The field of computer training encompasses several different areas. *Software vendor trainers* work for developer companies. *Consultants* work for themselves as independent contractors, often specializing in certain computer languages, skills, or platforms. Some trainers work in the corporate training departments of companies that develop products other than computers and software. Others are teachers and professors.

"As a software trainer, my duties are to be prepared to teach various topics related to our software to a variety of clients on any given day," says Marcy Anderson, a software trainer for Cyborg Systems, a human-resource software developer. "I teach from a training manual and demonstrate the procedures on my computer that displays the information on a large screen for the entire class. The class is given assignments throughout the day that they complete on their PCs. I assist them one on one with their questions as the class continues. Cyborg has a training center with four classrooms. I conduct classes in the training center, or I travel to the client and hold classes on-site."

Consultant trainers are certified to teach several different products, applications, environments, and databases, usually with companies such as Microsoft, IBM, or Apple. Most have been in the computer industry for many years, previously working as software programmers, architects, project managers, or developers.

Whatever their affiliation, most computer trainers use several ways to disseminate learning technologies, including CD-ROM, CBT-Text, electronic performance support systems, the Internet, intranets, multimedia presentations, and video conferencing.

Trainers are beginning to explore the field of online learning. In the article, "Our Turn-of-the-Century Trend Watch," Paul Clothier, senior instructor, Softwire Corporation, says, "Improved online learning (OL) design and technologies will significantly impact the technical training profession over the next few years. At present, much of the technical training taking place is in the form of instructor-led training (ILT) in a classroom. There are many advantages to ILT, but there are also considerable disadvantages, such as time investment, travel, and expense. To get a group of your most valuable technical people off to a week of training is often a major expense and inconvenience. Organizations are crying out for a better alternative, and OL increasingly is seen as an option."

REQUIREMENTS
High School
If you are interested in a career in computer training, take as many computer and mathematics classes as possible in high school. These will provide the foundation for the rest of your computer education. Start learning about computer programs, such as Visual Basic, on your own. Speech, drama, or other performance courses will also help get you used to speaking in front of a crowd. "A little showmanship doesn't hurt in keeping the class interested," notes Marcy Anderson.

Postsecondary Training
While there is no universally accepted way to prepare for a job in computer training, a bachelor's degree is generally required by most employers. The best major for this field is not set in stone, however. Some majors that share skills with training include computer science, business, and education. To teach some of the more complex systems, a graduate degree might be necessary.

"In my personal experience, I did not pursue an education degree to become a trainer," says Anderson. "I have a business degree and years of experience in the human resources field. For software training, though, knowledge of software and computers is essential. A degree in education would provide excellent skills for this type of position. Additionally, a business or liberal arts major might provide the presentation skills that are valuable. Certainly any presentation or public speaking certifications would be desirable."

Obtaining graduate and postgraduate degrees enhances potential marketability, as well as future salaries.

Certification or Licensing
As a trainer, you should be certified in the products (such as Microsoft C++, MFC, Visual Basic, and Access), developments (including Internet, HTML, Java Script), applications (MS Office, for example), environments (such as OS/2, Windows, client/server), and

databases (including ADO, Access, ODBC, BD/2, and SQL) you want to instruct. Classes in each of the disciplines are available from the manufacturers, and you must pass an examination before receiving certification. Trainers who are employed by hardware and software developers might receive on-the-job instruction on the most current product releases. Certification is not mandatory (except for consultants), but will provide you with a competitive advantage. ITrain, the International Association of Information Technology Trainers awards the professional technical trainer designation to association members who complete a seminar, submit a 30-minute video of one of their training presentations, and pay an application fee. Additionally, applicants must provide 10 student references and post-class evaluations. The American Society for Training and Development offers the certified professional in learning and performance designation to applicants who pass an examination.

Technological advances come so rapidly in the computer field that continuous study is necessary to keep your skills up to date. Continuing education is usually offered by employers, hardware and software vendors, colleges and universities, or private training institutions. Additional training can also come from professional associations.

Other Requirements

"Trainers need to be patient and extroverted," says Anderson. "A sense of humor is essential, along with a high level of energy. People who are very introverted, even though they might be good with computers, should not do software training." As a trainer, you will have to be ready to teach any class in your repertoire at any time, so you have to be adaptable and flexible to handle that uncertainty.

EXPLORING

One way to begin exploring this field now is to talk to someone who is a computer trainer. Marcy Anderson also suggests getting involved in speech or drama clubs. "Any experiences a high school student can get in making presentations or performing in front of a group help to build the skills necessary to be successful in this career," she says.

Internships are always helpful ways of obtaining some experience in the field before graduation. Working in the training department of a large corporation or software vendor would provide invaluable experience and contacts.

Teach yourself the various software packages, and read as much as you can about the industry. To stay updated in this field, read publications such as *Computer* magazine (http://www.computer. org/computer). Although jobs in the computer industry are abundant, there is always competition for desirable positions.

EMPLOYERS

Computer trainers work for a variety of employers, from large, international companies to community colleges. Many work for hardware and software manufacturers or training departments in the bigger companies. Others are employed by training companies that disseminate training information and tools. Still other computer trainers work independently as consultants. The rest are employed by schools, adult continuing education programs, and government institutions. Some software companies and consultants operate training sites on the Internet. Since almost every type of company will require computer training at one point or another, these companies are located throughout the country and, indeed, throughout the world.

STARTING OUT

There are several ways to obtain a position as a computer trainer. Some people are hired right out of college by software companies. "There are many software companies that hire smart college grads to work with clients and implement their software," notes Marcy Anderson. Others start out in technical positions with software companies and then move into training as their expertise in the product increases.

Job candidates for computer trainer positions might obtain their jobs from on-campus recruitment, classified want ads, posting their resumes on the Internet, or word of mouth. Many large cities hold technology job fairs that host hundreds of companies, all of which are interested in hiring.

ADVANCEMENT

Computer trainers can move upward into positions such as training specialists, senior training specialists, and training managers, depending on the size of the company.

EARNINGS

In general, computer trainers' salaries increase with the level of their education and the amount of their experience. According to a 2007 salary survey conducted by the Redmond Media Group, the average salary of the responding Microsoft Certified Trainers (MCTs) was $82,322. These figures do not include yearly bonuses, which may add several thousand dollars to a trainer's income. Additionally, these salaries are for MCTs, so not all computer trainers will have incomes in this range. For example, Salary.com reports that technical trainers earned salaries that ranged from less than $41,115 to $78,058 or more in 2008. In addition to education and experience, other factors influencing earnings are the size of the employer and, if the trainer is working independently, the number of clients he or she has during the year.

Most computer trainers who are employed by corporations receive medical and dental insurance, paid vacations, sick days, and retirement plans. Some companies also offer reimbursement for continuing education courses and training.

WORK ENVIRONMENT

Computer trainers normally work in offices in comfortable surroundings. They usually work 40 hours a week, which is the same as many other professional or office workers. However, travel to clients' sites can be required and might increase the number of hours worked per week. They spend most of their time in classrooms or training facilities. "The best part of the job is that it is interesting and fun," says Marcy Anderson. "It is nice to be an 'expert' and impart knowledge to others, even though it can be hard sometimes to feel up and energized to teach every day."

OUTLOOK

There will be a great need for computer trainers in the coming years as computer technology continues to develop. Information from the EQW National Employer Survey indicates that employers are using a variety of external training providers. As this outsourcing grows, an increase in the number of training providers is likely. Such independent providers as community and technical colleges, universities, profit-oriented learning and development centers, and private industry associations will all be discovering new business opportunities in outsourcing, according to the ASTD. "The short life cycles of technological products, compounded by the greater complexity of many job roles, are expected to heighten the demand for external information-technology education providers and other training providers," the ASTD notes.

FOR MORE INFORMATION

For information on certification and career resources, contact
American Society for Training and Development
1640 King Street, Box 1443
Alexandria, VA 22313-2043
Tel: 703-683-8100
http://www.astd.org

For information on certification, contact
ITrain, International Association of Information Technology Trainers
PMB 616
6030-M Marshalee Drive
Elkridge, MD 21075-5987
Tel: 888-290-6200
http://itrain.org

Education Directors and Museum Teachers

QUICK FACTS

School Subjects
English
History
Speech

Personal Skills
Communication/ideas
Helping/teaching

Work Environment
Primarily indoors
One location with some
  travel

Minimum Education Level
Bachelor's degree

Salary Range
$18,000 to $40,000 to
  $57,734+

Certification or Licensing
None available

Outlook
More slowly than the average

DOT
099

GOE
12.03.04

NOC
5124

O*NET-SOC
N/A

OVERVIEW

People visit museums, zoos, and botanical gardens to learn and observe. *Education directors,* or *curators of education,* are responsible for helping these people enrich their visits. Education directors plan, develop, and administer educational programs at museums and other similar institutions. They plan tours, lectures, and classes for individuals, school groups, and special interest groups.

Museum teachers also provide information, share insights, and offer explanations of exhibits. Direct communication ranges from informal explanations at staff previews of a new exhibit, to addressing corporate donor groups, to aiding groups of schoolchildren. Museum teachers may write exhibit labels, prepare catalogs, or contribute to multimedia installations. Museum teachers also teach by demonstration, by conducting studio classes, or by leading field trips.

HISTORY

Long ago, churches displayed art and furnishings for worshipers to view. The early equivalents of education directors were the priests or laypeople who developed expertise in these collections. As public museums grew, so did their need for education directors. When Europeans began to encourage the idea of universal education, museums began to draw in visitors who needed to be taught about their collections.

Similarly, zoos and arboretums, which were originally organized to exhibit their animals and plants to experts, began to teach others about their collections. Education directors were hired to plan programs and tours for visitors.

In the United States, early museums displayed objects relating to colonial history. Some were in former homes of wealthy colonists and others were established at the first U.S. universities and colleges. In these early museums *curators* or *archivists* maintained the collections and also explained the collections to visitors. As the collections grew and more visitors and groups of visitors came, education directors were hired by the curators to coordinate educational programs.

THE JOB

Education directors carry out the educational goals of a museum, zoo, botanical garden, or other similar institution. The educational goals of most of these institutions include nurturing curiosity and answering questions of visitors, regardless of age or background. Education directors work with administrators and museum or zoo boards to determine the scope of their educational programs. Large museums may offer full schedules of classes and tours, while smaller ones may only provide tours or lectures at the request of a school or other group.

Education directors plan schedules of courses to be offered through the zoo or museum. They may hire lecturers from local colleges or universities as well as regular educational staff members to lead tours or discussion groups. Education directors are usually responsible for training the staff members and may also work with professionals or university faculty to determine the content of a particular lecture, class, or series of lectures. They prepare course outlines and establish the credentials necessary for those who will teach the courses.

In smaller institutions the education director may do much of the teaching, lecturing, or tour leading. In zoos, the education director can arrange for small children to watch cows being milked or for the children to pet or feed smaller animals such as goats. In museums, the education director's job often depends on the museum's collection. In art museums, visitors are often older than in natural history museums, and the education director may plan programs that allow older children to explore parts of the collection at their own pace.

Education directors often promote their programs on local radio or television or in newspapers. They may speak to community or school groups about the museum's education department and encourage the groups to attend. Sometimes, education directors deliver lectures or offer classes away from the museum or zoo.

The education director is responsible for the budget for all educational programs. Directors prepare budgets and supervise the records of income and spending. Often, schools or other groups are charged lower rates for tours or classes at museums or zoos. Education directors work with resource coordinators to establish budgets for resource materials. These need to be updated regularly in most institutions. Even in natural history museums, where the collections may change less than in other museums, slide collections may need to be updated or presentations altered if new research has led to different interpretations of the objects. The education director may also prepare grant proposals or help with fund-raising efforts for the museum's educational program. Once a grant has been received or a large gift has been offered to the education department, the education director plans for the best use of the funds within the department.

Education directors often work with exhibit designers to help create displays that are most effective for visitors. They may also work with illustrators to produce illustrations or signs that enhance exhibits. Zoos, for example, often display maps near the animals to show their countries of origin.

Education directors train their staff members as well as volunteers to work with individual visitors and groups. Some volunteers may be trained to assist in presentations or to help large groups on tours. It is the responsibility of the education director to see that the educational program is helpful and interesting to all of those who visit the museum or zoo.

Special activities planned by education directors vary widely depending on the institution. Film programs, field trips, lectures, and full-day school programs may be offered weekly, monthly, or annually. Some zoos and arboretums have ongoing tours offered daily, while others may only give tours for prearranged groups.

In larger museums, education directors may have a staff of educators. Museum teachers may serve as *docents* or *interpreters* who interact directly with visitors. Docents also give prepared talks or provide information in a loosely structured format, asking and answering questions informally. Good content knowledge is required, as well as sensitivity to visitor group composition and the ability to convey information to different types of audiences. Scholarly researchers, for example, have a different knowledge base and attention span than children.

A museum teacher at the Virginia War Museum helps a young boy
try on a cap worn by members of the U.S. military in the Gulf War.
(Jeff Greenberg, The Image Works)

Other museum teachers, such as *storytellers,* may be self-employed
people who contract with a museum to provide special programs a few
times a year. Many teachers are volunteers or part-time workers.

Education specialists are experts in a particular field, which
may be education itself or an area in which the museum has large
holdings, such as Asian textiles, North American fossils, or pre-
Columbian pottery. Education specialists divide their time between
planning programs and direct teaching. They may supervise other
teachers, conduct field trips, or teach classes in local schools as part
of joint programs of study between museums and schools.

Educational resource coordinators are responsible for the collection of education materials used in the educational programs. These
may include slides, posters, videotapes, DVDs, books, or materials
for special projects. Educational resource coordinators prepare, buy,
catalog, and maintain all of the materials used by the education
department. They sometimes have a lending library of films, videos,
DVDs, books, or slides that people may borrow. Resource coordinators keep track of the circulation of materials. They may also lead
tours or workshops for educators or school personnel to teach them
about the collection of the museum or zoo and to keep them apprised

of new materials the educators may use in their tours or in their own classrooms. Resource coordinators and directors attend conventions and teachers' meetings to promote their institution's educational program and to encourage participation in their classes or tours.

REQUIREMENTS

High School

As an education director or a museum professional, you will need a diverse educational background to perform well in your job. At the high school level, you should take courses in creative writing, literature, history of world civilizations, American history, the sciences, foreign language, art, and speech. These courses will give you general background knowledge you can use to interpret collections, write letters to school principals, design curriculum materials, develop multicultural education, and lecture to public audiences. Math and computer skills are also strongly recommended. You will use these skills when preparing budgets and calculating the number of visitors that can fit in an exhibit space, and when writing grants or asking corporations and federal agencies for program funding.

Postsecondary Training

Education directors must have a bachelor's degree. Many museums, zoos, and botanical gardens also require a master's degree. The largest zoos and museums prefer to hire education directors who have doctoral degrees.

Some colleges in the United States offer programs of instruction leading to a degree in museology (the study of museums). Most education directors work in museums that specialize in art, history, or science. These directors often have degrees in fields related to the museum's specialty. Those who work in zoos usually have studied biology or zoology or have worked closely with animals. Education directors who work in more specialized museums often have studied such specialized fields as early American art, woodcarvings, or the history of circuses. As an education director, you must have a good working knowledge of the animals, plants, or artifacts in the collection.

Museum teachers and education specialists must also have a bachelor's degree in an academic discipline or in education.

Other Requirements

Excellent communication skills are essential in this field. Your primary responsibility will be to interpret and present collections to a broad public audience. The ability to motivate and teach many individuals from a wide range of cultural backgrounds, age groups, and educational levels is necessary. You should also be organized and flexible. You will be at a great advantage if you know a foreign language, sign language, and/or CPR.

EXPLORING

If you are interested in becoming an education director or museum teacher, volunteer experience should be easy to obtain. Most zoos and museums have student volunteers. You can request a position in the education department where you may help with elementary school tours, organize files or audiovisual materials, or assist a lecturer in a class.

College-preparatory courses are important if you are interested in this field. Apply to colleges or universities with strong liberal arts programs. Courses in art, history, science, and education are recommended if you want to work at museums. Courses in biology, zoology, botany, and education are beneficial if you wish to work at zoos or botanical gardens. Some larger zoos and museums offer internships to college students who are interested in the field.

The American Association of Museums publishes an annual museum directory, a monthly newsletter, and a bimonthly magazine. It also publishes *Careers in Museums: A Variety of Vocations* and *Museums: A Place to Work: Planning Museum Careers. Introduction to Museum Work,* published by the American Association for State and Local History, discusses the educational programs at various museums. The American Public Gardens Association publishes a directory of more than 700 internships offered through public gardens each year. (See the end of this article for contact information.)

EMPLOYERS

Institutions with a primary goal to educate the public about their collections hire education directors. Depending on each institution's monetary resources, most museums, large and small, zoos, botanical gardens, and occasionally historical societies employ education directors to ensure public access to their collections. Institutions with small operating budgets or limited visitor access sometimes hire part-time educators or rely on volunteer support.

STARTING OUT

Your first job in a museum or zoo will likely be as a teacher or resource coordinator working in the education department. With a few years of experience and improved understanding of the institution's collection, you may enter competition for promotion to education director. Many people in the field transfer from one museum to another or from one zoo to another, in order to be promoted to the position of education director.

ADVANCEMENT

Once in the education department, most people learn much of their work on the job. Experience in working with different people and groups becomes very important. Education directors must continually improve their understanding of their own institution's collection so that they can present it to school and other groups in the best way possible. Some education directors work for the federal government in specific subject areas such as aeronautics, philately (the study of postage stamps and related materials), science, or technology. They must be proficient in these fields as well as in education.

Museum teachers with experience and appropriate academic or teaching credentials may become content specialists in one area of the museum's collection or may become a director of education, assuming responsibility for the departmental budget, educational policies and community outreach programs, and training and supervision of numerous staff and volunteer workers. Advancement may depend on acquisition of an advanced degree in education or in an academic field. Because professional supervisory positions are few in comparison to the large corps of teachers, museum teachers desiring advancement may need to look beyond their home institution, perhaps accepting a smaller salary at a smaller museum in return for a supervisory title.

Teachers who leave museum work are well positioned to seek employment elsewhere in the nonprofit sector, especially with grant-funding agencies involved in community-based programs. In the for-profit sector, excellent communication skills and the ability to express an institution's philosophy both in writing and in interviews are skills valued by the public relations departments of corporations.

EARNINGS

Salaries for education directors vary widely depending on the size, type, and location of the institution, as well as the education and experience of the director. According to Salary.com, 50 percent of education specialists who were employed at museums earned between $36,885 and $50,414 in 2008. Salaries ranged from less than $31,887 to $57,734 or more annually. Museum teachers can expect to earn from $18,000 to $22,000 to start. Those with experience earn from $25,000 to $35,000 or more. Fringe benefits, including medical and dental insurance, paid vacations and sick leave, and retirement plans, vary according to each employer's policies.

Fringe benefits, including medical and dental insurance, paid vacations and sick leave, and retirement plans, vary according to each employer's policies.

WORK ENVIRONMENT

Most people who choose to be education directors like to be in museums, botanical gardens, or zoos. They also enjoy teaching, planning activities, organizing projects, and carrying a great deal of responsibility. Those in zoos usually enjoy animals and like being outdoors. Those in museums like the quiet of a natural history museum or the energy and life of a science museum designed for children. Education directors should enjoy being in an academic environment where they work closely with scholars, researchers, and scientists.

Education directors in larger institutions usually have their own offices where they do planning and other administrative work, but they spend the majority of their time in other parts of the museum and at other locations where they lead education programs.

Most museum teachers have a base of operation in the museum but may not have a private office, since the bulk of their work is carried out in exhibit areas, in resource centers or study rooms within the museum, in classrooms outside of the museum, or in the field. Permanent staff work a normal workweek, with occasional weekend or evening assignments.

Museum teaching varies from day to day and offers innovative teachers a chance to devise different programs. However, museum teaching is different from conventional classroom teaching where educators have the benefit of more time to convey ideas and facts.

OUTLOOK

Employment for education directors and museum teachers is expected to grow more slowly than average for all occupations through the next decade, according to the U.S. Department of Labor. Budget cutbacks have affected many museums and other cultural institutions, which have in turn reduced the size of their education departments. Museums in the United States have seen significant reduction in the number of visitors, which is directly related to the slowdown in the travel industry.

Many educators with specialties in sciences, the arts, or zoology are interested in becoming education directors at museums and zoos. Competition is especially intense for positions in large cities and those with more prestigious reputations. Some smaller museums and botanical gardens may cut out their education director position altogether until the economic climate improves, or they may get by with part-time education directors.

FOR MORE INFORMATION

For information about publications, meetings, seminars, and workshops, contact
American Association for State and Local History
1717 Church Street
Nashville, TN 37203-2991
Tel: 615-320-3203
http://www.aaslh.org

For a directory of museums and other information, contact
American Association of Museums
1575 Eye Street, NW, Suite 400
Washington, DC 20005-1113
Tel: 202-289-1818
http://www.aam-us.org

For a directory of internships offered through public gardens, contact
American Public Gardens Association
100 West 10th Street, Suite 614
Wilmington, DE 19801
Tel: 302-655-7100
http://www.publicgarden.org

Elementary School Teachers

OVERVIEW

Elementary school teachers instruct students from the first through sixth or eighth grades. They develop teaching outlines and lesson plans, give lectures, facilitate discussions and activities, keep class attendance records, assign homework, and evaluate student progress. Most teachers work with one group of children throughout the day, teaching several subjects and supervising such activities as lunch and recess. Approximately 1.5 million elementary school teachers are employed in the United States.

HISTORY

The history of elementary education can be traced back to about 100 B.C., when the people of Judah established schools for young children as part of their religious training.

In the early days of Western elementary education, the teacher only had to have completed elementary school to be considered qualified to teach. There was little incentive for an elementary school teacher to seek further education. School terms were generally short (about six months) and buildings were often cramped and poorly heated. Many elementary schools combined the entire eight grades into one room, teaching the same course of study for all ages. In these earliest schools, teachers were not well paid and had little status or recognition in the community.

When people began to realize that teachers should be better educated, schools designed to train teachers, called normal schools,

QUICK FACTS

School Subjects
English
Speech

Personal Skills
Communication/ideas
Helping/teaching

Work Environment
Primarily indoors
Primarily one location

Minimum Education Level
Bachelor's degree

Salary Range
$30,370 to $45,570 to $72,720+

Certification or Licensing
Required

Outlook
Faster than the average

DOT
092

GOE
12.03.03

NOC
4142

O*NET-SOC
25-2021.00

were established. The first normal school was private and opened in Concord, Vermont, in 1823. The first state-supported normal school was established in Lexington, Massachusetts, in 1839. By 1900, nearly every state had at least one state-supported normal school.

The forerunner of the present-day college or school of education in large universities was the normal department established at Indiana University in 1852. Since that time, normal schools have given way to teachers' colleges and today almost every university in the country has a school or college of education.

THE JOB

Depending on the school, elementary school teachers teach grades one through six or eight. In smaller schools, grades may be combined. There are still a few one-room, one-teacher elementary schools in remote rural areas. However, in most cases, teachers instruct approximately 20–30 children of the same grade. They teach a variety of subjects in the prescribed course of study, including language, science, mathematics, and social studies. In the classroom, teachers use various methods to educate their students, such as reading to them, assigning group projects, and showing films for discussion. Teachers also use educational games to help their pupils come up with creative ways to remember lessons.

In the first and second grades, elementary school teachers cover the basic skills: reading, writing, counting, and telling time. With older students, teachers instruct history, geography, math, English, and handwriting. To capture attention and teach new concepts, they use arts and crafts projects, workbooks, music, and other interactive activities. In the upper grades, teachers assign written and oral reports and involve students in projects and competitions such as spelling bees, science fairs, and math contests. Although they are usually required to follow a curriculum designed by state or local administrators, teachers study new learning methods to incorporate into the classroom, such as using computers to surf the Internet.

"I utilize many different, some unorthodox, teaching tools," says Andrea LoCastro, a sixth-grade teacher in Clayton, New Jersey. "I have a lunchtime chess club. Students give up their recess to listen to classical music and play, or learn to play, chess." She has also found that role-playing activities keep her students interested in the various subjects. "We are studying ancient Greece," she says, "and I currently have my students writing persuasive essays as either part of Odysseus' legal team or the Cyclops' legal team. I intend to culminate the activity with a mock trial, Athenian style."

An elementary school teacher goes over a lesson with some of his students. *(Rhoda Sidney, The Image Works)*

To create unique exercises and activities such as those LoCastro uses, teachers need to devote a fair amount of time to preparation outside of the classroom. They prepare daily lesson plans and assignments, grade papers and tests, and keep a record of each student's progress. Other responsibilities include communicating with parents through written reports and scheduled meetings, keeping their classroom orderly, and decorating desks and bulletin boards to keep the learning environment visually stimulating.

Elementary school teachers may also teach music, art, and physical education, but these areas are often covered by specialized teachers. *Art teachers* develop art projects, procure supplies, and help students develop drawing, painting, sculpture, mural design, ceramics, and other artistic abilities. Some art teachers also teach students about the history of art and lead field trips to local museums. *Music teachers* teach music appreciation and history. They direct organized student groups such as choruses, bands, or orchestras, or guide music classes by accompanying them in singing songs or playing instruments. Often, music teachers are responsible for organizing school pageants, musicals, and plays. *Physical education teachers* help students develop physical skills such as coordination, strength, and stamina and social skills such as self-confidence and good sportsmanship. Physical education teachers often serve as sports coaches and may organize field days and intramural activities.

When working with elementary-aged children, teachers need to cultivate students' social skills along with general school subjects. They serve as disciplinarians, establishing and enforcing rules of conduct to help students learn right from wrong. To keep the classroom manageable, teachers maintain a system of rewards and punishments to encourage students to behave, stay interested, and participate. In cases of classroom disputes, teachers must also be mediators, teaching their pupils to peacefully work through arguments.

Recent developments in school curricula have led to new teaching arrangements and methods. In some schools, one or more teachers work with students within a small age range instead of with particular grades. Other schools are adopting bilingual education, where students are instructed throughout the day in two languages by either a *bilingual teacher* or two separate teachers.

Many teachers find it rewarding to witness students develop and hone new skills and adopt an appreciation for learning. In fact, many teachers inspire their own students to later join the teaching profession themselves. "Teaching is not just a career," says LoCastro, "It is a commitment—a commitment to the 20-plus children that walk into your classroom door each September eager for enlightenment and fun."

REQUIREMENTS

High School

Follow your school's college preparatory program and take advanced courses in English, mathematics, science, history, and government to prepare for an education degree. Art, music, physical education, and extracurricular activities will contribute to a broad base of knowledge necessary to teach a variety of subjects. Composition, journalism, and communications classes are also important for developing your writing and speaking skills.

Postsecondary Training

All 50 states and the District of Columbia require public elementary education teachers to have a bachelor's degree in either education or in the subject they plan to teach. Prospective teachers must also complete an approved training program. In the United States, there are more than 500 accredited teacher education programs, which combine subject and educational classes with work experience in the classroom.

Though programs vary by state, courses cover how to instruct language arts, mathematics, physical science, social science, art, and music. Additionally, prospective teachers must take educational training courses, such as philosophy of education, child psychology, and learning methods. To gain experience in the classroom, student teachers are placed in a school to work with a full-time teacher. During this training period, student teachers observe the ways in which lessons are presented and the classroom is managed, learn how to keep records of attendance and grades, and gain experience in handling the class, both under supervision and alone.

Some states require prospective teachers to have master's degrees in education and specialized technology training to keep them familiar with more modern teaching methods using computers and the Internet.

Certification or Licensing

Public school teachers must be licensed under regulations established by the state in which they are teaching. If they relocate, teachers have to comply with any other regulations in their new state to be able to teach, though many states have reciprocity agreements that make it easier for teachers to change locations.

Licensure examinations test prospective teachers for competency in basic subjects such as mathematics, reading, writing, teaching, and other subject matter proficiency. In addition, many states are moving towards a performance-based evaluation for licensing. In this case, after passing the teaching examination, prospective teachers are given provisional licenses. Only after proving themselves capable in the classroom are they eligible for a full license.

Another growing trend spurred by recent teacher shortages is alternative licensure arrangements. For those who have a bachelor's degree but lack formal education courses and training in the classroom, states can issue a provisional license. These workers immediately begin teaching under the supervision of a licensed educator for one to two years and take education classes outside of their working hours. Once they have completed the required coursework and gained experience in the classroom, they are granted a full license. This flexible licensing arrangement has helped to bring additional teachers into school systems needing instructors.

Other Requirements

Many consider the desire to teach to be a calling. This calling is based on a love of children and a dedication to their welfare. If you want to become a teacher, you must respect children as individuals, with personalities, strengths, and weaknesses of their own. You must also be patient and self-disciplined to manage a large group independently. Teachers make a powerful impression on children, so they need to serve as good role models. "Treat students with kindness and understanding, rules and consequences," LoCastro suggests. "Be nice, yet strict. They'll love you for it."

EXPLORING

To explore the teaching career, look for leadership opportunities that involve working with children. You might find summer work as a counselor in a summer camp, as a leader of a scout troop, or as an assistant in a public park or community center. Look for opportunities to tutor younger students or coach children's athletic teams. Local community theaters may need directors and assistants for summer children's productions. Day care centers often hire high school students for late afternoon and weekend work.

EMPLOYERS

There are approximately 1.5 million elementary school teachers employed in the United States. Teachers are needed at public and private institutions, including parochial schools and Montessori schools, which focus more on the child's own initiatives. Teachers are also needed in day care centers that offer full-day elementary programs and charter schools, which are smaller, deregulated schools that receive public funding. Although rural areas maintain schools, more teaching positions are available in urban or suburban areas.

STARTING OUT

After obtaining a college degree, finishing the student teaching program, and becoming certified, prospective teachers have many avenues for finding a job. Career services offices in colleges and state departments of education maintain listings of job openings. Many local schools advertise teaching positions in newspapers. Another option is directly contacting the administration in the schools in which you'd like to work. While looking for a full-time position, you can work as a substitute teacher. In more urban areas with many schools, you may be able to find full-time substitute work.

ADVANCEMENT

As teachers acquire experience or additional education, they can expect higher wages and more responsibilities. Teachers with leadership skills and an interest in administrative work may advance to serve as principals or supervisors, though the number of these positions is limited and competition is fierce. Others may advance to work as *senior* or *mentor teachers* who assist less experienced staff. Another move may be into higher education, teaching education classes at a college or university. For most of these positions, additional education is required.

Other common career transitions are into related fields. With additional preparation, teachers can become librarians, reading specialists, or counselors.

"I intend to continue teaching as my career," says Andrea LoCastro. "I am not at all interested in moving up to administration. I will, however, pursue a master's in teaching after receiving tenure."

EARNINGS

According to the U.S. Department of Labor, the median annual salary for elementary school teachers was $45,570 in 2006. The lowest 10 percent earned $30,370 or less; the highest 10 percent earned $72,720 or more. Private school teachers generally earn less than public school teachers.

According to the American Federation of Teachers, beginning teachers earned an average salary of $31,753 a year in 2004–05.

Teachers often supplement their earnings by teaching summer classes, coaching sports, sponsoring a club, or other extracurricular work. More than half of all teachers belong to unions such as the American Federation of Teachers or the National Education Association. These unions bargain with schools over contract conditions such as wages, hours, and benefits. Depending on the state, teachers usually receive a retirement plan, sick leave, and health and life insurance. Some systems grant teachers sabbatical leave.

WORK ENVIRONMENT

Most teachers are contracted to work 10 months out of the year, with a two-month vacation during the summer. During their summer break, many continue their education to renew or upgrade their teaching licenses and earn higher salaries. Teachers in schools that operate year-round work eight-week sessions with one-week breaks in between and a five-week vacation in the winter.

Teachers work in generally pleasant conditions, although some older schools may have poor heating or electrical systems. The work can seem confining, requiring them to remain in the classroom throughout most of the day. Although the job is not overly strenuous, dealing with busy children all day can be tiring and trying. Teachers must stand for many hours each day, do a lot of talking, show energy and enthusiasm, and may have to handle discipline problems. But, according to Andrea LoCastro, problems with students are usually overshadowed by their successes. "Just knowing a child is learning something because of you is the most rewarding feeling, especially when you and the child have struggled together to understand it."

OUTLOOK

According to the *Occupational Outlook Handbook,* employment opportunities for elementary school teachers are expected to grow slightly faster than the average for all occupations through 2016. The need to replace retiring teachers will provide many opportunities nationwide.

The demand for teachers varies widely depending on geographic area. Inner-city schools characterized by poor working conditions and low salaries often suffer a shortage of teachers. In addition, more opportunities exist for those who specialize in a subject in which it is harder to attract qualified teachers, such as mathematics, science, bilingual education, or foreign languages.

The National Education Association believes it will be a difficult challenge to hire enough new teachers to meet rising enrollments and replace the large number of retiring teachers, primarily because of low teacher salaries. Higher salaries along with other necessary changes, such as smaller classroom sizes and safer schools, will be necessary to attract new teachers and retain experienced ones. Other challenges for the profession involve attracting more men into teaching. The percentage of male teachers continues to decline.

The demand for teachers varies widely depending on geographic area. The U.S. Department of Labor predicts that the following states will experience the largest increases in enrollment: Nevada, Arizona, Texas, and Georgia. Enrollments in the Midwest will remain steady, while enrollments in the Northeast will decline.

In order to improve education, drastic changes are being considered by some districts. Some private companies are managing public schools in the hope of providing better facilities, faculty, and equipment. Teacher organizations are concerned about taking school management away from communities and turning it over to remote corporate headquarters.

Charter schools and voucher programs are two other controversial alternatives to traditional public education. Publicly funded charter schools are not guided by the rules and regulations of traditional public schools. Some view these schools as places of innovation and improved educational methods; others see them as ill-equipped and unfairly funded with money that could better benefit local school districts. Vouchers, which exist only in a few cities, use public tax dollars to allow students to attend private schools. In theory, the vouchers allow for more choices in education for poor and minority students. Teacher organizations see some danger in giving public funds to unregulated private schools.

FOR MORE INFORMATION

For information about careers, education, and union membership, contact the following organizations

American Federation of Teachers
555 New Jersey Avenue, NW
Washington, DC 20001-2029
Tel: 202-879-4400
Email: online@aft.org
http://www.aft.org

National Council for Accreditation of Teacher Education
2010 Massachusetts Avenue, NW, Suite 500
Washington, DC 20036-1023
Tel: 202-466-7496
Email: ncate@ncate.org
http://www.ncate.org

National Education Association
1201 16th Street, NW
Washington, DC 20036-3290
Tel: 202-833-4000
http://www.nea.org

This Web site serves as a clearinghouse for men interested in becoming teachers.

MenTeach
http://www.menteach.org

INTERVIEW

Jessica Weil is a physical education teacher in Topeka, Kansas. She discussed her career with the editors of Careers in Focus: Education.

Q. How long have you been a physical education teacher?
A. This will be the start of my eleventh year teaching physical education (PE) to elementary students, kindergarten through sixth grade. I teach in a school district that has six elementary schools. This is my fourth year of teaching physical education full time at Wanamaker Elementary and, since we have to have

two or sometimes two-and-a-half classes at a time in PE, I team-teach with another certified PE teacher.

Q. Why did you decide to become a physical education teacher?

A. I decided to become a physical education teacher during some of my undergraduate classes that actually had us learning and participating in physical education activities and games that weren't just sports. It was nothing like the physical education I grew up with. Back then, we did whatever sport was in season at the time, and the "athletes" excelled and the "non-athletes" hated every minute of it. The activities we were learning in our college courses made physical activities fun for anyone, and the goal was to teach the students to keep active for a lifetime. That made so much sense to me, and I couldn't understand why all physical educators didn't agree with that. I was going to be a physical education teacher who was there to educate all students, and not just use it as a recruiting tool for the high school athletic teams.

Q. Can you take us through a day in your life as a physical education teacher?

A. My day starts with getting equipment out that I will be using for that day or week. Every morning I have bus duty. I help the students get off the bus and into the school. My first period class is third grade. I work really hard the first few weeks of school so that the procedures of class are automatic and the students know what is expected of them. I have a lesson plan every day, which is great. I have not always had that at other schools where I have worked. I have fourth and fifth grade before lunch and then sixth, second, first, and kindergarten. I am fortunate to have the lower elementary grades close together, which makes it a lot easier when using equipment and planning for the day. The end of the day is spent putting equipment away because the gym is usually used after school for athletics or after-school programs.

Q. What advice would you give to high school students who are interested in this career?

A. My advice to future physical educators is do it because you love it. Unfortunately, I see a lot of people in my profession that get into teaching PE because they want to be a "coach." Coaching can be a nice complement to teaching, but teaching should always be first. My second piece of advice is to join clubs and/or organizations that support your future goals.

Q. What are the three most important professional qualities for physical education teachers?

A. The most important quality for a physical education teacher is flexibility. Any teacher will tell you that you don't just teach when you work with elementary students. Schedules change often due to field trips, assemblies, surprise fire drills, weather, anytime someone needs to use your gym in a moment's notice. You may never get through that great lesson plan that you prepared because of some unforeseen event like classes arriving late, someone getting a bloody nose, or a parent note that has been written in crayon. These are also the things that make the job interesting and challenging.

Another important quality is having a positive attitude. It is always important to remember why you are teaching. If there is a policy or incident that arises the first question I ask myself is, "Is this what is best for my students?" Sometimes policies, situations, schedules, etc. would make life easier for teachers and administrators, but do absolutely nothing to help the students. It is important that we are always advocates for our students. We want to make learning a positive experience. If you are happy or at least portray happiness, it will be contagious and your students will like you and your class. If they are comfortable in class, they will ask more questions and hopefully learn more.

The third most important quality of a physical education teacher is organizational skill. Organization is important, especially if you have large classes. You have to make sure you have enough equipment and that it is placed properly around the gym or outside area so your class will run smoothly and efficiently. You only have your students for a certain amount of time and you want to get the maximum participation you can during that short time. Smooth transition from activity to activity is vital as well, because again you don't want any wasted minutes if you can help it.

English as a Second Language (ESL) Teachers

QUICK FACTS

School Subjects
English
Social studies

Personal Skills
Communication/ideas
Helping/teaching

Minimum Education Level
Bachelor's degree

Salary Range
$24,610 to $43,910 to
$75,680+

Certification or Licensing
Required for certain positions

Outlook
Faster than the average

DOT
N/A

GOE
N/A

NOC
N/A

O*NET-SOC
25-3011.00

OVERVIEW

English as a second language (ESL) teachers specialize in teaching people of all ages the English language. Their students may be immigrants, refugees, children of foreign-born parents, or children who may be living in a home where English is not spoken as the primary language.

HISTORY

Less than four centuries ago, no more than a few million people spoke English. Today, it is the primary language of more than 370 million people, and is spoken as a second language by tens of millions of others. English is considered necessary to conduct international business, and people everywhere choose to speak English in order to communicate. However, English is considered one of the most difficult languages to learn, primarily because of its many irregularities. It has a larger vocabulary than any other language and incorporates numerous slang terms and newly coined words and phrases.

Although English has been taught in the American school systems for decades, ESL instructors have emerged with the arrival of more immigrants and refugees, as well as more children being born to non-English-speaking parents.

According to the Census Bureau's 2006 American Community Survey, the estimated foreign-born population of the United States was nearly 37.5 million. In 50.7 million households, a language other than English is spoken and 19.5 million people speak English less than "very well." This trend is likely to continue, which will increase the demand for ESL teachers. According to the National Center for Education Statistics, the demand for placement in ESL classes has grown and there is a long waiting list for ESL classes in many parts of the country.

THE JOB

Today, many public and private schools employ teachers trained as ESL instructors. ESL teachers do not usually speak the language of the students they teach. However, many teachers try to learn some key words and phrases in their students' native tongues in order to communicate better. ESL teachers teach English usage and pronunciation, as well as core language skills necessary for students to participate in other classes such as math and science, and in order to interact socially with other students.

According to Linda Lahann, an ESL instructor in Iowa with more than 20 years of experience, students may not have a good background in reading in their own native language. In some countries, reading skills are not encouraged. "Not having a good reading base makes it even more difficult to learn the language in a new country," says Lahann.

The primary goal of ESL teachers is to help students learn to use the English language to communicate both verbally and in writing. They also try to build students' confidence through instruction and interaction. It is important to encourage students to become involved in social activities. Lahann says that it is very rewarding to watch her students participate in extracurricular activities and see them embrace the English language and American culture.

Classroom methods may include games, videos, DVDs, computers, field trips, role-playing, and other activities to make learning fun and interesting for students. Classes often center on teaching conversation skills, telephone skills, the art of listening, and the idioms of the English language. The instructor helps the students learn correct pronunciation, sentence structure, communication skills, and vocabulary.

As any other teacher, ESL teachers prepare lesson plans and exams, keep student records, and fulfill other assignments as required by the school system. They keep current in the field by reading books and researching new teaching methods. Many states require teachers to take college-level courses to maintain their teaching certificates.

ESL teachers may work with immigrants or refugees, and children of parents who may have immigrated and not learned the English language. In some homes, English is not spoken as the primary language, which makes it difficult for the child to relate to peers and teachers when entering school. Those who teach in border states will be more likely to teach immigrant students.

ESL teachers may also teach refugees who have witnessed the tragedies of war. "Not only do I deal with language," says Lahann, "but I must also deal with the students' emotions and their experiences with culture shock. Many of these refugees have seen and experienced war." Lahann, who has taught students from 21 different countries, says that there are many different levels of understanding that her students go through. She says for some students, it may take three to five years of ESL classes until they reach the point where they can compete academically. "The most special thing, though, is watching the light bulb come on," she says. "You see that they have finally broken the code. That makes it all worthwhile."

Many ESL teachers teach adults in basic education programs. With the increase of refugees and immigrants to the United States, community centers, libraries, churches and other religious entities, and assistance centers are offering ESL classes as well. Some immigration and refugee assistance centers and organizations may offer classes in learning the English language as part of their programs.

Teaching adults requires skills that are different than those required to teach young people. Frequently, adults are not comfortable being back in a learning environment, so teachers may have to help them develop study habits and regain their confidence in the classroom. In addition, many adult students have jobs and may have families to care for, so teachers must be aware of the other commitments students might have and be able to adjust their teaching methods and expectations.

ESL instructors might be hired by a company to provide instruction to its workers as a part of the company's employee training or employee assistance programs, or simply as a courtesy to its workers. Classes might be held during break or lunch or after work hours. The class may also be a required part of the employee's workday.

Simply because of the nature of the job, ESL teachers may get emotionally involved with their students. "I am often invited to participate in cultural celebrations in the community as well as family events such as weddings," says Lahann. "It is exciting and rewarding to be a part of their social and family life as well."

Many communities have a strong networking system that involves churches, schools, health providers, resettlement programs, and other groups. ESL instructors may get involved with these groups and make visits to the students' homes to meet their families. They sometimes work with translators to communicate with the families

An ESL teacher (left) shows a student how to make a particular sound. *(Marty Heitner, The Image Works)*

and students. Some school systems and community programs also use translators to help the families communicate with medical providers, social workers, and government officials.

ESL instructors also find many opportunities overseas teaching English as a foreign language (EFL).

REQUIREMENTS

High School

While in high school, courses in English, foreign language, and social studies will help build your knowledge of languages and different cultures. Joining a Spanish, French, German, or other language club is a good way to immerse yourself in a different language than your own. Better yet, become a foreign exchange student or host a student from another country. Participate in community multicultural events and volunteer at community relocation centers. Many churches also have refugee assistance programs that can offer excellent exposure to helping people from other countries.

Postsecondary Training

Teaching certificate requirements vary by state. There are about 500 accredited teacher education programs in the United States and most are designed to meet the requirements of the state in which they are located. The National Council for Accreditation of Teacher Education provides information on teacher education programs. Some states may require that prospective teachers pass a test before being admitted to an education program.

While a college major in ESL is fairly new, there are some programs that offer such specialized degrees. Students may choose to major in ESL or major in education with a concentration in ESL as a subject area. Student teaching is almost always required in a teaching program. Prospective teachers are placed in a school with a full-time teacher to observe the class, learn how to prepare lesson plans, and actually work with students and other teachers.

Besides licensure and courses in education, teachers at the secondary level usually need 24–36 hours of college work in ESL-related classes. Some states may require a master's degree.

ESL teachers of adult students do not need an education degree or a license. There are a variety of training programs available for ESL teachers of adults. These programs usually last from four to 12 weeks and upon successful completion, a diploma or certificate is awarded.

Certification or Licensing

Teachers in public schools must be licensed under regulations established by the Department of Education of the state in which they teach. Not all states require licensure for teachers in private or parochial schools. Prospective ESL teachers should check the specific requirements of the state where they plan to teach.

In addition to becoming certified to teach, many teachers become certified in ESL or bilingual education. Forty-four states and the District of Columbia offer ESL teacher certification or endorsement. Visit http://www.ncela.gwu.edu/expert/faq/09certif.html for a list of state certification requirements. According to a 2001 survey of state education agencies conducted by the National Clearinghouse for English Language Acquisition, there are approximately 48,791 teachers certified in ESL and 40,108 teachers certified in bilingual education. There is an average of one teacher certified in ESL for every 44 limited English proficient (LEP) students and one teacher certified in bilingual education for every 47 LEP students.

Some states require continuing education courses in order to maintain teaching certificates. Overseas employers of ESL teachers may also require a certificate and prior teaching experience.

Other Requirements

To be a successful ESL teacher, you must be patient and have the ability to relate to people of other nationalities and cultures. You should have an interest in the history and traditions of other countries and nationalities. An ability to relate to people from all walks of life is also necessary to be successful as an ESL teacher.

ESL instructors who teach adults should be aware of the different ways people absorb information and be able to adapt their teaching skills to successfully teach older students.

EXPLORING

There are many ways of exploring a career in ESL. Get involved with people of different cultures through community service, school activities, or religious programs. If possible, travel to other countries and learn first-hand about other cultures. Speak to ESL teachers about their teaching methods and how they adjust their teaching approach to reach students who have limited English language skills. Volunteer to help with any assistance, relocation, or referral programs that your community or religious organization might have for immigrants or refugees.

EMPLOYERS

Teachers are needed at public and private schools, including parochial schools and vocational schools. Depending on the size of the school, its geographic location, and the number of students in need of assistance, some schools may hire teachers primarily as ESL instructors. Other schools may hire them to teach different subjects in addition to ESL classes. Larger cities and areas of refugee relocation and large immigrant populations provide the most ESL job opportunities.

Some community-based and government assistance programs may hire ESL teachers. Many adult education teachers are self-employed and work on a contract basis for industries, community and junior colleges, universities, community organizations, job training centers, and religious organizations. Relocation services might also hire ESL teachers on a contract or part-time basis.

Overseas employers hire ESL teachers, usually for short-term assignments. Many people become ESL teachers because it allows them to earn a living while seeing the world and experiencing other cultures.

STARTING OUT

After completing the required certification program for the state in which they want to teach, ESL teachers can use their college career services office to find a teaching position. State departments of

Facts About the English Language

- Approximately 20 percent of people on earth speak English with some competence.
- More than one billion people worldwide are currently learning English.
- More than 80 percent of Web pages are in English.
- How many words are in the English language? This is difficult to answer, but the unabridged *Oxford English Dictionary* has about 600,000 words.
- The average native English speaker knows approximately 12,000 to 20,000 words, but only uses about 10 percent of these words in daily communication.
- What's the longest English word? Antidisestablishmentarianism.

Source: EnglishEnglish.com

education also may have listings of job openings. Most major newspapers list available teaching positions in their classified ad sections. Teaching organizations such as the National Education Association and the American Federation of Teachers also list teaching opportunities. Prospective teachers can also apply directly to the principals or superintendents of the schools in which they would like to teach. Finally, substitute teaching can provide experience as well as possible job contacts.

Contacting schools or community assistance programs, as well as adult education programs, may provide some job opportunities. College professors might have job hunting suggestions as well as helpful contacts in the field.

ADVANCEMENT

Advancement opportunities into educational administrative positions or corporate or government training positions may be available for those instructors with advanced degrees.

Lateral moves are also common in school systems. For instance, an ESL teacher may transfer to a position as a counselor or choose to teach another subject. Other opportunities may be available within community- and government-based programs that assist refugees and immigrants.

EARNINGS

The U.S. Department of Labor reports that the median salary of adult literacy and remedial education teachers was $43,910 in 2006. Earnings ranged from $24,610 to more than $75,680 a year. Teachers employed at elementary and secondary schools had mean annual earnings of $53,050 in 2006. Private school teachers on average earn less than public school teachers.

Most teachers join the American Federation of Teachers or the National Education Association. These unions bargain on behalf of the teachers regarding contract conditions such as wages, hours, and benefits. Depending on the state, teachers usually receive a retirement plan, sick leave, and health and life insurance. Some schools may grant sabbatical leave.

Overseas employers usually offer low pay, but they sometimes offer housing, airfare, medical care, or other benefits as part of the teaching contract.

WORK ENVIRONMENT

Many ESL teachers work in primary and secondary classrooms. While the job is not physically strenuous, it can be tiring and trying. Some school environments can be tense if drugs, gangs, and other problems are present. Although there has been increased media coverage of school violence, reports indicate that it has actually decreased over the years.

Traditional classroom teachers work a typical school day, but most put in extra hours preparing for classes and meeting other teaching duty requirements. If other duties require sponsorship of clubs or coaching, teachers may have to work some nights or weekends. They may also be required to be at the school extra hours to accommodate parent and student meetings.

Teachers who teach adult education classes or other community-based classes may be required to hold classes at night to accommodate students' work and family schedules. Some ESL teachers may hold classes in corporate classrooms, libraries, or meeting rooms as well as at local colleges or schools. The facilities and locations can vary.

Just as there is a large demand for ESL instructors in the United States, there is also a need for ESL educators overseas. Opportunities to teach abroad exist in traditional classrooms or on military bases overseas. Teachers may be required to work in less than desirable settings depending on the culture and the economics of the area.

OUTLOOK

According to the U.S. Department of Labor, employment of ESL teachers will grow slightly faster than the average for all occupations through 2016. There will be a continuing need for ESL teachers of adults through the next decade because of the increasing number of immigrants and other non-English speakers entering this country, particularly in California, Florida, Texas, and New York. Opportunities will also be good in parts of the Midwest and plains states, as these areas have recently begun to attract large numbers of immigrants. Jobs will be available in school systems, community and social service agencies, and at community colleges.

FOR MORE INFORMATION

For salary statistics and general information on teaching careers, contact
American Federation of Teachers
555 New Jersey Avenue, NW
Washington, DC 20001-2029
Tel: 202-879-4400
Email: online@aft.org
http://www.aft.org

This organization has information on adult ESL literacy and offers resources and support for teachers, tutors, and others interested in the education of refugees, immigrants, and other U.S. residents whose native language is other than English.
Center for Adult English Language Acquisition
4646 40th Street, NW
Washington, DC 20016-1859
Tel: 202-355-1500
http://www.cal.org/caela

For statistics on English-language acquisition, contact
National Clearinghouse for English Language Acquisition
The George Washington University
Graduate School of Education and Human Development
2121 K Street, NW, Suite 260
Washington, DC 20037-1861
Tel: 800-321-6223
Email: askncela@gwu.edu
http://www.ncela.gwu.edu

For information on accredited teacher education programs, contact
National Council for Accreditation of Teacher Education
2010 Massachusetts Avenue, NW, Suite 500
Washington, DC 20036-1023
Tel: 202-466-7496
Email: ncate@ncate.org
http://www.ncate.org

*For additional information on ESL and teaching careers, contact
the following organizations:*
National Education Association
1201 16th Street, NW
Washington, DC 20036-3290
Tel: 202-833-4000
http://www.nea.org

Teachers of English to Speakers of Other Languages
700 South Washington Street, Suite 200
Alexandria, VA 22314-4287
Tel: 703-836-0774
Email: info@tesol.org
http://www.tesol.org

Guidance Counselors

OVERVIEW

Guidance counselors provide a planned program of guidance services for all students, principally in junior and senior high schools. In addition to helping students to plan for college and careers, guidance counselors listen to students' problems, advise students, and help them develop coping skills and learn to become good problem-solvers and decision-makers on their own.

Although guidance counselors often meet with students individually, they may also work with groups, organizing several students for special meetings to address a problem or issue that the students have in common. There are approximately 260,000 educational, vocational, and school counselors employed in the United States.

HISTORY

Counseling in secondary schools, as a comprehensive guidance service, is an outgrowth of the earlier program of vocational guidance in schools. Such programs were slowly adopted by school systems through the 1920s—Boston and New York being among the first—but during the Depression years, school budgets were at a low point and the vocational guidance movement came to a standstill.

After World War II, guidance services began to show signs of growth. Many factors contributed to the sudden spurt. There was a great migration from rural to urban living, and city schools became overcrowded. Students lost their individual identities in the crowds of fellow students. More courses were being offered in more schools, and choices were difficult to make. Changes in careers because of

82

technological developments made it difficult for parents to help their children with wise career choices. Living standards improved, and more parents, who themselves had most often not gone to college, planned a college education for their children. In the years following World War II, school guidance programs grew both in number and in expanded fields. Many colleges and universities initiated training programs for guidance counselors, and licensure standards for counselors were established or upgraded. The U.S. Office of Education embarked upon an ambitious leadership program for guidance services as the need for professionals in the field increased.

THE JOB

Guidance counselors work in a school setting to provide a planned program of guidance services for the benefit of all students enrolled in the school. The guidance program is not one single plan, but is the combination of many related activities. It has several aims, but its most important one is to help each student in the process of growth toward maturity. The guidance program is designed to help students achieve independence.

All guidance programs are unique. Each one is built especially for the school in which it functions. Guidance counselors confer with parents, with professional personnel such as school psychologists, social workers, and health officers, and with other faculty and staff members to assure a totally effective school program. They meet with students on an appointment, walk-in, or teacher-referral basis to talk about students' personal problems or concerns; to review academic, attendance, or conduct records; or to discuss anything else that may be an issue to the students, faculty, or parents.

Jim Buist is a middle school counselor. "I work with about 800 young people during a highly charged transitional period of their lives," he says. "My primary role as a school counselor is to aid these young people in a successful educational process." This involves a number of tasks: scheduling (matching students with teachers and courses); testing (to monitor progress); and counseling (to guide young people through the troubles of adolescence).

Students seek out Buist's advice on such subjects as family issues, peer pressure, alcohol/drug problems, the development of romantic relationships, and illness and death. "Besides working with the students themselves," Buist says, "I have the obligation and opportunity to work with other professionals as teams or supports, as well as with parents who are often looking for the manual that was supposed to come with their children."

In addition to dealing directly with students, guidance counselors collect and organize materials for students to read about such topics as peer pressure, self-esteem, occupations, and post-high school educational opportunities. They conduct group guidance meetings in which topics of special concern or interest to the age-group involved are discussed. For example, they may direct an orientation program for students new to the school. In addition, they organize, administer, score, and interpret the school's standardized testing program.

Guidance counselors assist students in choosing their courses of studies, developing more effective study habits, and making tentative choices regarding goals for the future. They help students in selecting the post-high school training that will best meet their educational and vocational needs. They also assist students in applying for admission to colleges or vocational schools, help locate scholarships, and write reference letters to college admissions officers or prospective employers.

Guidance counselors plan, organize, and conduct events such as career days and college days. They may conduct follow-up studies of students who have left school or graduated, requesting their help in evaluating the curriculum in light of their postsecondary work experiences.

Guidance counselors also conduct in-service education courses for other faculty members or speak at meetings of interested members of the community. They refer students with problems that are beyond the scope of the school to address, to such community resources as social welfare agencies, child guidance clinics, health departments, or other services.

REQUIREMENTS

High School

Enroll in a college preparatory curriculum to prepare for the college degrees required of guidance counselors. You should take courses in humanities, social studies, and psychology. Courses in mathematics are important, because mathematical and statistical theory underlie much of the standardized testing program. You should take English and speech courses because both written and spoken communication with students, parents, and administrators are important components to this occupation.

Postsecondary Training

The basic requirement for a school counselor in many states is a bachelor's degree and certain stipulated courses at the graduate level. As an undergraduate, you'll probably major in education so that you'll have the course work necessary for teacher certification. About six in 10 counselors hold master's degrees. The American Counseling Association (ACA) and the American School Counselor Association provide information to students when selecting graduate programs in counselor education.

To get accepted into a graduate program, you'll have to have a bachelor's degree and possibly a teaching certificate and a few years teaching experience. These programs usually require at least two years of additional study, as well as an internship. Course subjects include career development, group counseling, substance abuse counseling, art therapy, and grief and loss counseling.

Certification or Licensing

You must be certified by your state to work as a counselor; the requirements for certification vary from state to state. Most state licensure standards require that counselors have teaching experience. This experience may be as short as one year or as long as two to three years. Some states also require that counselors have work experience outside of the teaching field.

The NBCC offers the national certified counselor (NCC) designation as well as the national certified school counselor (NCSC) designation. In order to apply for the NCC, you must have earned a master's degree with a major study in counseling and you must pass the National Counselor Examination. NCCs are certified for a period of five years. In order to be recertified, they must complete 100 contact clock hours of continuing education or pass the examination again. In order to receive the NCSC credential, you must complete the above requirements, gain field experience in school counseling as a graduate student, and then complete two years of post-master's supervised school counseling. Many states require some type of credentialing or certification for counselors, and all states require those who work in school settings to be certified.

Other Requirements

Your most important asset will be your ability to relate easily and well to others. To achieve a sound relationship with other adults and with children, you must have a sincere interest in other people and their welfare. You must be able to relate to all kinds of people and situations, and to be sensitive to issues of race, religion, sexual orientation, and disability. Jim Buist lists empathy, patience, and listening skills among the personal qualities of a good counselor. He emphasizes that counselors should have some teaching experience in their background. Without that experience, Buist says, "you'll be missing the experience that you'll need day in and day out. It would be difficult, if not impossible, to learn these skills on the job."

EXPLORING

Your best resource for information about work as a guidance counselor is right in your own high school. Ask your school's counselor how he or she got started in the career, and about the nature of the job. You may even be allowed to assist your counselor with a variety of projects like career days, or college recruitment. With your counselor's help, you can identify some of the particular issues affecting your fellow students and come up with ways to address the issues with special projects. You can also get a sense of a counselor's job by working on the school newspaper. As a reporter, you'll have the opportunity to interview students, get to know their concerns, and write editorials about these issues.

The ACA publishes a great deal of information about the field of professional guidance. The ACA's Web site (http://www.counseling. org) features many articles about counseling; the ACA also produces a monthly publication called *Counseling Today.* An electronic version, called *CT Online,* is available at its Web site.

EMPLOYERS

Approximately 250,000 educational, vocational, and school counselors are employed in the United States. Counselors are employed in elementary, middle, and high schools all across the country. They work in both public and private schools. Though counselors are considered important to a school system, not every school has its own counselor on staff. Some counselors have offices in more than one school; for example, they may work for both a middle school and a high school, or they may work for other schools in the district.

STARTING OUT

While some students do enroll in master's programs immediately after finishing their undergraduate programs, most experts advise that you get at least a few years of teaching experience under your belt before you pursue a master's degree in counselor education. Some people work for several years as teachers before considering a degree in school counseling. College professors and advisers should be able to direct you to sources of counseling positions. Some state boards of education maintain job lines, as do many public school districts. These jobs are also advertised in the newspaper.

The ACA lists job openings across the country in its publication *Counseling Today,* and on the ACA's Web site. The American School Counselor Association offers professional development programs to help members expand skills, attain knowledge, and access networking opportunities.

ADVANCEMENT

Schools with more than one counselor on the staff offer the opportunity for staff members to advance to *school guidance director.* The title may be misleading, however, as one does not usually "direct" the program; rather, one coordinates it. The school principal is usually the actual director of the program. Most advancement within the guidance counselor position will be in the form of wage increases.

Some counselors with many years of experience may be appointed as *guidance coordinator* or *director* for a city or county school system. Their duties usually include program development.

For the most part, counselors are promoted to positions outside of counseling itself, such as to administration or supervisory jobs. Some counselors obtain advanced degrees and become college or university teachers. Jim Buist has had many opportunities to move into administrative positions, but has turned them down. "I know I would miss the contact with the students, parents, and teachers," he says.

EARNINGS

Wages for guidance counselors vary by region of the country, school and district size, and age of the students. Larger districts typically offer higher salaries, and counselors working with high school students tend to earn more than counselors for younger grades. According to the U.S. Department of Labor, the median salary for educational, vocational, and school counselors was $47,530 in 2006. Earnings ranged from less than $27,240 to $75,920 or more.

Because guidance counselors work on an academic calendar, they typically get a good amount of vacation time, especially in the summer. Some counselors use this time to take additional university courses. Counselors receive the benefits and pension plans provided by the school or district that employs them.

WORK ENVIRONMENT

Most guidance counselors have a private office in which to talk with students, parents, and faculty members. But they also work in other parts of the school, leading presentations, coordinating events, and speaking to classes of students. Counselors find it rewarding to help students through their problems, and to help them plan for their futures, but they also have the stress of guiding young people through difficult times. "This is an age where a counselor/teacher can make a difference," Jim Buist says.

Guidance counselors usually work more than 40 hours a week, spending a part of each day in conferences and meetings. They often arrive at school earlier than do many other staff members and may return to the school in the evening to talk with parents who are unable to come to the school during working hours.

OUTLOOK

The U.S. Department of Labor predicts that the employment of counselors will increase about as fast as the average rate for all occupations through 2016. State legislation requiring counselors at the elementary school level and increasing duties for counselors at all levels will ensure continued demand for workers in this field.

Though violence in the schools has been decreasing, some students are afraid to go to school. This fear may be a result of the rash of shootings and gang-related violence that plagued some schools in the late 1990s. The federal government has called for more counselors in the schools to help address issues of violence and other dangers, such as drug use. The government, along with counseling professionals, is also working to remove the stigma of mental illness and to encourage more children and families to seek help from school counselors. To keep schools safe, guidance counselors may be more actively involved in instituting and maintaining discipline policies.

Technology will continue to assist counselors in their jobs. With Internet access in school libraries and in career centers, counselors can easily direct students to specific career information, scholarship applications, and college Web sites. School counselors may also follow the lead of Internet counselors and offer guidance online; students seeking anonymity can request information and advice from their counselors through email and other online services.

FOR MORE INFORMATION

For information about current issues in counseling and graduate school programs, contact
American Counseling Association
5999 Stevenson Avenue
Alexandria, VA 22304-3304

Tel: 800-347-6647
http://www.counseling.org

For information about membership, publications, and professional development programs, contact
American School Counselor Association
1101 King Street, Suite 625
Alexandria, VA 22314-2957
Tel: 800-306-4722
Email: asca@schoolcounselor.org
http://www.schoolcounselor.org

For information about college admission counseling and a list of several related publications, contact
National Association for College Admission Counseling
1631 Prince Street
Alexandria, VA 22314-2818
Tel: 703-836-2222
Email: info@nacacnet.org
http://www.nacac.com

For information on certification, contact
National Board for Certified Counselors
3 Terrace Way
Greensboro, NC 27403-3660
Tel: 336-547-0607
Email: nbcc@nbcc.org
http://www.nbcc.org

INTERVIEW

Michelle Camp is an academic advisor at Norview High School in Norfolk, Virginia. She discussed her career with the editors of Careers in Focus: Education.

Q. How long have you worked in the field? Why did you decide to pursue this career?

A. I have been an academic adviser for eight and a half years. Previous to being an academic adviser, I was employed as a teacher. My teaching career took off in New York, as a teacher of English. I was employed for 10 years there before moving to Virginia. I landed a job as a reading specialist and continued on that track for nine years. It was during this time that I realized that I spent a large portion of time listening to young people. Oftentimes, they would ask for my opinion on a particular matter. I found myself learning and understanding many things about teenagers. I often thought about how I could better serve them. It was at that point that I realized that I could better serve them as a guidance counselor.

Q. Tell us about a typical day in your life on the job.

A. A typical day usually begins with a few early bird students who are in dire need to get to me first. After they are off to class, I begin sending for students to hold individual academic sessions with them. This consists of us talking about how they are doing in their classes and designing a program of study that will take them to their ultimate career goal. We discuss things that might get in the way of their success and how to avoid those traps. I share with them information about what colleges and scholarship committees, the military, and the work force are looking for. My students who are coming back from suspension must see me before going back to class. At predesignated times, I visit classrooms to hold small group sessions dealing with the everyday concerns of a high school student: grades, promotion, goals, college, credit sheets, etc. Senior students always have special needs. I spend a lot of time assisting them with colleges and scholarship applications, career choices, and offering suggestions on what they need to do to graduate on time. I assist parents with their concerns and act as a liaison between the teachers and parents. Each day brings new challenges. I have only given you a nutshell view of the work that an academic adviser does here at Norview High School on any given day.

Q. What do you like most and least about your job?

A. I like my students the most. If it were not for them, I would not be needed. My students are the reason why I do not mind getting up in the morning. They bring me so much joy.

The thing that I like the least about what I do is the paper work. There is so much of a paper trail that one can get lost in it. Some of it is necessary, but the majority of it is not.

Q. What are the three most important professional qualities for academic advisers?

A. The three most important professional qualities for an academic adviser are:

- It is most important to have a love for all children regardless of race, creed, color, learning abilities, or anything else that would seem to set preferences.
- Believe in what you do! Believe that you can make a difference, one child at a time.
- Listening is a key in effective counseling. We should listen twice as much as we speak.

Q. What advice would you give to high school students who are interested in this career?

A. There are several things that I would share with young people looking to go into school counseling. First of all, they must love young people of all ages. I would recommend that they prepare themselves by working towards an academic diploma, take higher-level classes, take a psychology or sociology class if offered, and maintain a good grade point average. I would also recommend that they consider joining a future teachers/educators club and perhaps getting involved with the Girl's or Boy's State or any other leadership program that their high school may offer.

Interpreters and Translators

QUICK FACTS

School Subjects
English
Foreign language
Speech

Personal Skills
Communication/ideas
Helping/teaching

Work Environment
Primarily indoors
Primarily multiple locations

Minimum Education Level
Bachelor's degree

Salary Range
$26,264 to $40,000 to
$100,000

Certification or Licensing
Recommended

Outlook
Much faster than the average

DOT
137

GOE
01.03.01

NOC
5125

O*NET-SOC
27-3091.00

OVERVIEW

An *interpreter* translates spoken passages of a foreign language into another specified language. The job is often designated by the language interpreted, such as Spanish or Japanese. In addition, many interpreters specialize according to subject matter. For example, *medical interpreters* have extensive knowledge of and experience in the health care field, while *court* or *judiciary interpreters* speak both a second language and the "language" of law. *Interpreters for the deaf* aid in the communication between people who are unable to hear and those who can.

In contrast to interpreters, *translators* focus on written materials, such as books, plays, technical or scientific papers, legal documents, laws, treaties, and decrees. A *sight translator* performs a combination of interpreting and translating by reading printed material in one language while reciting it aloud in another.

In the United States, approximately 41,000 interpreters and translators currently work full time.

HISTORY

Until recently, most people who spoke two languages well enough to interpret and translate did so only on the side, working full time in some other occupation. For example, many diplomats and high-level government officials employed people who were able to serve as interpreters and translators, but only as needed. These employees spent the rest of their time assisting in other ways.

Interpreting and translating have emerged as full-time professions only recently, partly in response to the need for high-speed communication across the globe. The increasing use of complex diplomacy has also increased demand for full-time translating and interpreting professionals. For many years, diplomacy was practiced largely between just two nations. Rarely did conferences involve more than two languages at one time. The League of Nations, established by the Treaty of Versailles in 1919, established a new pattern of communication. Although the "language of diplomacy" was then considered to be French, diplomatic discussions were carried out in many different languages for the first time.

Multinational conferences have been commonplace since the early 1920s. Trade and educational conferences are now held with participants of many nations in attendance. Responsible for international diplomacy after the League of Nations dissolved, the United Nations now employs many full-time interpreters and translators, providing career opportunities for qualified people. In addition, the European Union employs a large number of interpreters.

THE JOB

Although interpreters are needed for a variety of languages and different venues and circumstances, there are only two basic systems of interpretation: simultaneous and consecutive. Spurred in part by the invention and development of electronic sound equipment, simultaneous interpretation has been in use since the charter of the United Nations (UN).

Simultaneous interpreters are able to convert a spoken sentence instantaneously. Some are so skilled that they are able to complete a sentence in the second language at almost the precise moment that the speaker is conversing in the original language. Such interpreters are usually familiar with the speaking habits of the speaker and can anticipate the way in which the sentence will be completed. The interpreter may also make judgments about the intent of the sentence or phrase from the speaker's gestures, facial expressions, and inflections. While working at a fast pace, the interpreter must be careful not to summarize, edit, or in any way change the meaning of what is being said.

In contrast, *consecutive interpreters* wait until the speaker has paused to convert speech into a second language. In this case, the speaker waits until the interpreter has finished before resuming the speech. Since every sentence is repeated in consecutive interpretation, this method takes longer than simultaneous interpretation.

In both systems, interpreters are placed so that they can clearly see and hear all that is taking place. In formal situations, such as those at the UN and other international conferences, interpreters are often assigned to a glass-enclosed booth. Speeches are transmitted to the booth, and interpreters, in turn, translate the speaker's words into a microphone. Each UN delegate can tune in the voice of the appropriate interpreter. Because of the difficulty of the job, these simultaneous interpreters usually work in pairs, each working 30-minute shifts.

All international conference interpreters are simultaneous interpreters. Many interpreters, however, work in situations other than formal diplomatic meetings. For example, interpreters are needed for negotiations of all kinds, as well as for legal, financial, medical, and business purposes. Court or judiciary interpreters, for example, work in courtrooms and at attorney–client meetings, depositions, and witness-preparation sessions.

Other interpreters serve on call, traveling with visitors from foreign countries who are touring the United States. Usually, these language specialists use consecutive interpretation. Their job is to make sure that whatever the visitors say is understood and that they also understand what is being said to them. Still other interpreters accompany groups of U.S. citizens on official tours abroad. On such assignments, they may be sent to any foreign country and might be away from the United States for long periods of time.

Interpreters also work on short-term assignments. Services may be required for only brief intervals, such as for a special conference or single interview with press representatives.

While interpreters focus on the spoken word, translators work with written language. They read and translate novels, plays, essays, nonfiction and technical works, legal documents, records and reports, speeches, and other written material. Translators generally follow a certain set of procedures in their work. They begin by reading the text, taking careful notes on what they do not understand. To translate questionable passages, they look up words and terms in specialized dictionaries and glossaries. They may also do additional reading on the subject to understand it better. Finally, they write translated drafts in the target language.

REQUIREMENTS

High School

If you are interested in becoming an interpreter or translator, you should take a variety of English courses, because most translating work is from a foreign language into English. The study of one or more foreign languages is vital. If you are interested in becoming proficient in one or more of the Romance languages, such as Italian, French, or Spanish, basic courses in Latin will be valuable.

While you should devote as much time as possible to the study of at least one foreign language, other helpful courses include speech, business, cultural studies, humanities, world history, geography, and political science. In fact, any course that emphasizes the written and/or spoken word will be valuable to aspiring interpreters or translators. In addition, knowledge of a particular subject matter in which you may have interest, such as health, law, or science, will give you a professional edge if you want to specialize. Finally, courses in typing and word processing are recommended, especially if you want to pursue a career as a translator.

Postsecondary Training

Because interpreters and translators need to be proficient in grammar, have an excellent vocabulary in their chosen language, and have sound knowledge in a wide variety of subjects, employers generally require that applicants have at least a bachelor's degree. Scientific and professional interpreters are best qualified if they have graduate degrees.

In addition to language and field-specialty skills, you should take college courses that will allow you to develop effective techniques in public speaking, particularly if you're planning to pursue a career as an interpreter. Courses such as speech and debate will improve your diction and confidence as a public speaker.

Hundreds of colleges and universities in the United States offer degrees in languages. In addition, educational institutions now provide programs and degrees specialized for interpreting and translating. Georgetown University (http://www.georgetown.edu/departments/linguistics) offers both undergraduate and graduate programs in linguistics. Graduate degrees in interpretation and translation may be earned at the University of California at Santa Barbara (http://www.ucsb.edu), the University of Puerto Rico (http://www.upr.clu.edu), and the Monterey Institute of International Studies (http://www.miis.edu/languages.html). Many of these programs include both general and specialized courses, such as medical interpretation and legal translation.

Academic programs for the training of interpreters can be found in Europe as well. The University of Geneva's School of Translation and Interpretation (http://www.unige.ch/en) is highly regarded among professionals in the field.

Certification or Licensing

Although interpreters and translators need not be certified to obtain jobs, employers often show preference to certified applicants. Certification in Spanish, Haitian, Creole, and Navajo is also required for interpreters who are employed by federal courts. State and local courts often have their own specific certification requirements. The National Center for State Courts has more information on certification for these workers. Interpreters for the deaf who pass an examination may qualify for either comprehensive or legal certification by the Registry of Interpreters for the Deaf.

The U.S. Department of State has a three-test requirement for interpreters. These include simple consecutive interpreting (escort), simultaneous interpreting (court/seminar), and conference-level interpreting (international conferences). Applicants must have several years of foreign language practice, advanced education in the language (preferably abroad), and be fluent in vocabulary for a very broad range of subjects.

Foreign language translators may be granted certification by the American Translators Association (ATA) upon successful completion of required exams. ATA certification is available for translators who translate the following languages into English: Arabic, Croatian, Danish, Dutch, French, German, Hungarian, Japanese, Polish, Portuguese, Russian, and Spanish. Certification is also available for translators who translate English into the following languages: Chinese, Croatian, Dutch, Finnish, French, German, Hungarian, Italian, Japanese, Polish, Portuguese, Russian, Spanish, and Ukrainian.

Other Requirements

Interpreters should be able to speak at least two languages fluently, without strong accents. They should be knowledgeable of not only the foreign language but also of the culture and social norms of the region or country in which it is spoken. Both interpreters and translators should read daily newspapers in the languages in which they work to keep current in both developments and usage.

Interpreters must have good hearing, a sharp mind, and a strong, clear, and pleasant voice. They must be able to be precise and quick in their translation. In addition to being flexible and versatile in their work, both interpreters and translators should have self-discipline and patience. Above all, they should have an interest in and love of language.

Finally, interpreters must be honest and trustworthy, observing any existing codes of confidentiality at all times. The ethical code of interpreters and translators is a rigid one. They must hold private proceedings in strict confidence. Ethics also demands that interpret-

More College Students
Studying Foreign Languages

The number of college students studying foreign languages is at its highest level since 1960, according to a survey by the Modern Language Association of America (visit http://www.mla.org/2006_flenrollment survey to read the complete survey). Language course enrollments grew from 608,749 in 1960 to 1,522,770 in 2006. Here are the most popular foreign languages studied by college students in 2006:

Language	Enrollment	Increase Since 2002
1. Spanish	822,985	+10.3 percent
2. French	206,426	+2.2 percent
3. German	94,264	+3.5 percent
4. American Sign Language	78,829	+29.7 percent
5. Italian	78,368	+22.6 percent
6. Japanese	66,605	+27.5 percent
7. Chinese	51,582	+51.0 percent
8. Latin	32,191	+7.9 percent
9. Russian	24,845	+3.9 percent
10. Arabic	23,974	+126.5 percent
11. Ancient Greek	22,849	+12.1 percent
12. Biblical Hebrew	14,140	+0.3 percent
13. Portuguese	10,267	+22.4 percent
14. Modern Hebrew	9,612	+11.5 percent
15. Korean	7,145	+37.1 percent

ers and translators not distort the meaning of the sentences that are spoken or written. No matter how much they may agree or disagree with the speaker or writer, interpreters and translators must be objective in their work. In addition, information they obtain in the process of interpretation or translation must never be passed along to unauthorized people or groups.

EXPLORING

If you have an opportunity to visit the United Nations, you can watch the proceedings to get some idea of the techniques and responsibilities of the job of the interpreter. Occasionally, an international conference session is televised, and you can observe interpreters at work. You should note, however, that interpreters who work at these conferences are in the top positions of the vocation. Not everyone may aspire to such jobs. The work of interpreters and translators is usually less public, but not necessarily less interesting.

If you have adequate skills in a foreign language, you might consider traveling in a country in which the language is spoken. If you can converse easily and without a strong accent and can interpret to others who may not understand the language well, you may have what it takes to work as an interpreter or translator.

For any international field, it is important that you familiarize yourself with other cultures. You can even arrange to correspond regularly with a pen pal in a foreign country. You may also want to join a school club that focuses on a particular language, such as the French Club or the Spanish Club. If no such clubs exist, consider forming one. Student clubs can allow you to hone your foreign-language speaking and writing skills and learn about other cultures.

Finally, participating on a speech or debate team enables you to practice your public speaking skills, increase your confidence, and polish your overall appearance by working on eye contact, gestures, facial expressions, tone, and other elements used in public speaking.

EMPLOYERS

There are approximately 41,000 interpreters and translators working full time in the United States. Although many interpreters and translators work for government or international agencies, some are employed by private firms. Large import–export companies often have interpreters or translators on their payrolls, although these employees generally perform additional duties for the firm. International banks, companies, organizations, and associations often employ both interpreters and translators to facilitate communication. In addition, translators and interpreters work at publishing houses, schools, bilingual newspapers, radio and television stations, airlines, shipping companies, law firms, and scientific and medical operations.

While translators are employed nationwide, a large number of interpreters find work in New York and Washington, D.C. Among the largest employers of interpreters and translators are the United Nations, the World Bank, the U.S. Department of State, the Bureau of the Census, the CIA, the FBI, the Library of Congress, the Red Cross, the YMCA, and the armed forces.

Finally, many interpreters and translators work independently in private practice. These self-employed professionals must be disciplined and driven, since they must handle all aspects of the business such as scheduling work and billing clients.

STARTING OUT

Most interpreters and translators begin as part-time freelancers until they gain experience and contacts in the field. Individuals can apply for jobs directly to the hiring firm, agency, or organization. Many of these employers advertise available positions in the classified section of the newspaper or on the Internet. In addition, contact your college career services office and language department to inquire about job leads.

While many opportunities exist, top interpreting and translating jobs are hard to obtain since the competition for these higher profile positions is fierce. You may be wise to develop supplemental skills that can be attractive to employers while refining your interpreting and translating techniques. The United Nations (UN), for example, employs administrative assistants who can take shorthand and transcribe notes in two or more languages. The UN also hires tour guides who speak more than one language. Such positions can be initial steps toward your future career goals.

ADVANCEMENT

Competency in language determines the speed of advancement for interpreters and translators. Job opportunities and promotions are plentiful for those who have acquired great proficiency in languages. However, interpreters and translators need to constantly work and study to keep abreast of the changing linguistic trends for a given language. The constant addition of new vocabulary for technological advances, inventions, and processes keep languages fluid. Those who do not keep up with changes will find that their communication skills become quickly outdated.

Interpreters and translators who work for government agencies advance by clearly defined grade promotions. Those who work for other organizations can aspire to become chief interpreters or chief translators, or reviewers who check the work of others.

Although advancement in the field is generally slow, interpreters and translators will find many opportunities to succeed as freelancers. Some can even establish their own bureaus or agencies.

EARNINGS

Earnings for interpreters and translators vary depending on experience, skills, number of languages used, and employers. In government, trainee interpreters and translators generally begin at the GS-5 rating, earning from $26,264 to $34,139 a year in 2008. Those with a college degree can start at the higher GS-7 level, earning from $32,534 to $42,290. With an advanced degree, trainees begin at the GS-9 ($39,795 to $51,738), GS-10 ($43,824 to $56,973), or GS-11 level ($48,148 to $62,593).

Interpreters who are employed by the United Nations work under a salary structure called the Common System. In 2008, UN short-term interpreters (workers employed for a duration of 60 days or less) had daily gross pay of $494.50 (Grade I) or $322.50 (Grade II). UN short-term translators and revisers had daily gross pay of $197.10 (Translator I), $242.05 (Translator II), $286.80 (Translator III/Reviser I), $323.20 (Translator IV/Reviser II), or $359.60 (Reviser III).

The U.S. Department of Labor reports the following mean annual salaries for interpreters and translators by specialty in 2006: junior colleges, $45,800; general medical and surgical hospitals, $38,430; local government, $35,200; and elementary and secondary schools, $33,680.

Interpreters employed by nonprofit organizations had median annual incomes of $47,690 in 2006, according to *Compensation in Nonprofit Organizations 2006*, a report from Abbott, Langer & Associates.

Interpreters and translators who work on a freelance basis usually charge by the word, the page, the hour, or the project. Freelance interpreters for international conferences or meetings can earn between $300 and $500 a day from the U.S. government.

By the hour, freelance translators usually earn between $15 and $35; however, rates vary depending on the language and the subject matter. Book translators work under contract with publishers. These contracts cover the fees that are to be paid for translating work as well as royalties, advances, penalties for late payments, and other provisions.

Interpreters and translators working in a specialized field have high earning potential. According to the National Association of Judiciary Interpreters and Translators, the federal courts pay $305 per day for court interpreters. Most work as freelancers, earning annual salaries from $30,000 to $100,000 a year.

Interpreters who work for the deaf also may work on a freelance basis, earning anywhere from $12 to $40 an hour, according to the Registry of Interpreters for the Deaf. Those employed with an agency, government organization, or school system can earn up to $30,000 to start; in urban areas, $40,000 to $50,000 a year.

Depending on the employer, interpreters and translators often enjoy such benefits as health and life insurance, pension plans, and paid vacation and sick days.

WORK ENVIRONMENT

Interpreters and translators work under a wide variety of circumstances and conditions. As a result, most do not have typical nine-to-five schedules.

Conference interpreters probably have the most comfortable physical facilities in which to work. Their glass-enclosed booths are well lit and temperature controlled. Court or judiciary interpreters work in courtrooms or conference rooms, while interpreters for the deaf work at educational institutions as well as a wide variety of other locations.

Interpreters who work for escort or tour services are often required to travel for long periods of time. Their schedules are dictated by the group or person for whom they are interpreting. A freelance interpreter may work out of one city or be assigned anywhere in the world as needed.

Translators usually work in offices, although many spend considerable time in libraries and research centers. Freelance translators often work at home, using their own personal computers, modems, dictionaries, and other resource materials.

While both interpreting and translating require flexibility and versatility, interpreters in particular, especially those who work for international congresses or courts, may experience considerable stress and fatigue. Knowing that a great deal depends upon their absolute accuracy in interpretation can be a weighty responsibility.

OUTLOOK

Employment for interpreters and translators is expected to grow much faster than the average for all occupations through 2016, according to the U.S. Department of Labor. However, competition for available positions will be fierce. With the explosion of such technologies as the Internet, lightning-fast modems, and videoconferencing, global communication has taken great strides. In short, the world has become smaller, so to speak, creating a demand for professionals to aid in the communication between people of different languages and cultural backgrounds.

In addition to new technological advances, demographic factors will fuel demand for translators and interpreters. Although some immigrants who come to the United States assimilate easily with respect to culture and language, many have difficulty learning English. As immigration to the United States continues to increase, interpreters and translators will be needed to help immigrants function in an English-speaking society. According to Ann Macfarlane, past president of the American Translators Association, "community interpreting" for immigrants and refugees is a challenging area requiring qualified language professionals.

Another demographic factor influencing the interpreting and translating fields is the growth in overseas travel. Americans on average are spending an increasing amount of money on travel, especially to foreign countries. The resulting growth of the travel industry will create a need for interpreters to lead tours, both at home and abroad.

In addition to leisure travel, business travel is spurring the need for more translators and interpreters. With workers traveling abroad in growing numbers to attend meetings, conferences, and seminars with overseas clients, interpreters and translators will be needed to help bridge both the language and cultural gaps.

While no more than a few thousand interpreters and translators are employed in the largest markets (the federal government and international organizations), other job options exist. The medical field, for example, provides a variety of jobs for language professionals, translating such products as pharmaceutical inserts, research papers, and medical reports for insurance companies. There will also be strong demand for interpreters in health care settings such as hospitals, outpatient treatment centers, and large offices of physicians due to the steady increase in immigrants to the United States who do not speak English as their primary language. Opportunities exist for qualified individuals in law, trade and business, tourism, recreation, and the government. Interpreters and translators who are fluent in Middle Eastern and North African languages will have especially strong employment opportunities in government.

The U.S. Department of Labor predicts that employment growth will be limited for conference interpreters and literary translators.

FOR MORE INFORMATION

For information on careers in literary translation, contact
American Literary Translators Association
University of Texas–Dallas
800 West Campbell Road, Mail Station JO51

Richardson, TX 75080-3021
http://www.literarytranslators.org

For more on the translating and interpreting professions, including information on accreditation, contact
American Translators Association
225 Reinekers Lane, Suite 590
Alexandria, VA 22314-2875
Tel: 703-683-6100
Email: ata@atanet.org
http://www.atanet.org

For more information on court interpreting, contact
National Association of Judiciary Interpreters and Translators
1707 L Street, NW, Suite 507
Washington, DC 20036-4201
Tel: 202-293-0342
Email: headquarters@najit.org
http://www.najit.org

For information on interpreter training programs for working with the deaf, contact
Registry of Interpreters for the Deaf
333 Commerce Street
Alexandria, VA 22314-2801
Tel: 703-838-0030
Email: membership@rid.org
http://www.rid.org

Mathematics Teachers

OVERVIEW

Mathematics teachers generally work with students in middle school or high school. They lecture, direct discussions, and test students' knowledge with exams, essays, and homework assignments. Teachers also develop teaching outlines and lesson plans, facilitate activities, keep class attendance records, and evaluate student progress.

HISTORY

Greek mathematicians in the sixth century B.C. helped to establish some of the basic laws and principles that govern mathematics today. They applied reason to write up proofs supporting geometric theorems. These theories were written in simple generalized form, using variables to represent "unknowns." The Pythagorean theorem ($a^2 + b^2 = c^2$) is an example of early mathematical discovery.

Muslim mathematicians gave us the Arabic numbering system based on the number 10. This system was adopted by traveling traders and spread through Europe and eventually the Americas. Principles of geometry and trigonometry were further developed and applied to navigation and surveying, resulting in great advances in these areas.

Today, new discoveries are as common in mathematics as new problems. The current wide scope of math has led to many advances in science, technology, and computer science in the last century.

THE JOB

Many successful people credit their secondary school teachers with helping them discover their talents and abilities while guiding them into college, careers, and other endeavors. The primary responsibility of math teachers is to instruct students in grades seven through 12 in a specific math subject. Teachers may teach a traditional math subject, such as geometry, algebra, or trigonometry, or in an applied math area, such as information technology, statistics, or probability.

Many secondary schools are expanding their course offerings to serve the individual interests of their students more effectively. "School-to-work" programs, which are vocational education programs designed for high school students and recent graduates, involve lab work and demonstrations to prepare students for highly technical jobs. Though they will likely be assigned to one specific level in a subject area, secondary school teachers may be required to teach multiple levels. For example, a secondary school mathematics teacher may teach algebra to a class of ninth-graders one period and trigonometry to high school seniors the next.

In the classroom, math teachers rely on a variety of teaching methods. They spend a great deal of time lecturing, but they also facilitate student discussion and develop projects and activities to interest the students in the subject. They show films and videos, use computers and the Internet, and possibly even invite guest speakers. Aside from assigning the usual textbook problems, they may also assign presentations and other more creative projects to facilitate learning. Each individual area of math usually requires more than one teaching approach.

Outside the classroom, math teachers prepare lectures, lesson plans, and exams. They evaluate student work and calculate grades. In the process of planning their classes, math teachers read textbooks and workbooks to determine problem assignments; photocopy notes, articles, and other handouts; and develop grading policies. They also continue to study alternative and traditional teaching methods to hone their skills. Math teachers may prepare students for special events and conferences and prepare students for math competitions. Many also serve as sponsors to student organizations in their field, such as a math club. Secondary school teachers also have the opportunity for extracurricular work such as athletic coaching or drama coaching, and they may monitor students during lunch, break times, and study halls. They may also accompany student groups on field days and to competitions and events. In addition, math teachers attend faculty meetings, meet with parents, and may travel to state and national teacher conferences.

Mathematics teachers must keep their skills current and their teaching methods up to date. They may be required by state regulations to take continuing education courses and may have to pass periodic exams to prove their competency in the field. In a field as challenging as mathematics, teachers often explore their subject outside of the classroom as well, by conducting research or reading journals about the field.

REQUIREMENTS

High School

If you are interested in pursuing a career as a math teacher, prepare yourself by taking classes in algebra, geometry, trigonometry, and calculus in high school. If available, take advanced math classes in statistics, probability, and logic. Classes in speech and English composition courses are also helpful to develop your communication skills. You should also explore extracurricular activities that will further challenge your math skills, such as joining a math club. The more involved you are now, the better you'll look to future employers.

Postsecondary Training

There are more than 500 accredited teacher education programs in the United States. Most of these programs are designed to meet the certification requirements for the state in which they're located. Some states may require that you pass a test before being admitted to an education program. You may choose to major in mathematics while taking required education courses, or you may major in secondary education with a concentration in math. You'll probably have advisors in both math and education to help you select courses.

Practice teaching, also called student teaching, with a local school is usually required as part of the education program. To fulfill this requirement, you will be assigned to work with a full-time teacher for a period of time. During student teaching, you will observe the ways in which lessons are presented and the classroom is managed, learn how to keep records of such details as attendance and grades, and get actual experience in handling the class, both under supervision and alone.

Prospective high school teachers usually need 24 to 36 credit hours of college work in the subject they wish to teach. Some states require a master's degree; teachers with master's degrees can earn higher salaries. Private schools generally do not require an education degree.

Certification or Licensing

As a public school teacher, you must be licensed under regulations established by the department of education of the state in which you are teaching. Although requirements vary by state, most require a bachelor's degree and the completion of a state-approved education program. Certain courses and education credits must be fulfilled as part of these training programs, and some states may also require you to maintain a minimum grade point average or even obtain a master's degree in education before teaching. Technology training is also a part of many states' licensing requirements. Not all states require licensure for teachers in private or parochial schools.

When you have received your teaching degree, you may request that a transcript of your college record be sent to the licensure section of the state department of education. If you have met licensure requirements, you will receive a certificate and thus be eligible to teach in the public schools of the state. In some states, you may have to take a competency exam to prove your basic skills before teaching. If you move to another state, you will have to resubmit college transcripts as well as comply with any other regulations in the new state to be able to teach there.

Because of a current teacher shortage, many states offer alternative licensing programs for individuals with bachelor's degrees in a subject (such as math) who have not taken the required number of education courses. Individuals may begin teaching immediately under the supervision of a licensed teacher while taking education courses part time. After working for one or two years and taking the required courses, they can earn a license.

The National Board for Professional Teaching Standards offers voluntary certification for teachers. To earn certification, individuals must pass a written assessment evaluating their teaching knowledge. All states recognize national certification and may grant higher salaries and promotions to those who obtain it.

Other Requirements

To succeed as a math teacher, not only will you need to meet all the educational and licensure requirements, but you should also have the right personality for the job. You will need respect for young people and a genuine interest in their success in life. In teaching, patience is most certainly a virtue; adolescence can be a troubling time for children, and these troubles often affect behavior and classroom performance. You may find yourself frustrated and discouraged by students' reactions or lack of response to you as their teacher. During these times, it is important to keep a level head and be patient as you try to connect with and educate them.

You will be working with students who are at very impressionable ages; you should serve as a good role model. You should also be well organized, as you'll have to keep track of the work and progress of a number of different students.

EXPLORING

By attending your own high school math classes, you have already gained a good sense of the daily work of a math teacher. But the requirements of a teacher extend far beyond the classroom, so ask to spend some time with one of your teachers after school. Ask about their job, how they prepared for their career, and look at lecture notes and record-keeping procedures.

To get some direct teaching experience, volunteer for a peer tutoring program. Other teaching opportunities outside your school may exist in your community; look into coaching an athletic team at the YMCA, counseling at a summer camp, teaching a math course at a community center, or assisting with a community theater production. Regardless of what subject you teach, gaining this outside experience will give you a taste of what it feels like to instruct others.

Consider joining the Junior Engineering Technical Society (JETS). JETS promotes learning in mathematics, engineering, science, and technology. Visit its Web site at http://www.jets.org. You may also find it helpful to read publications about this field and visit Web sites such as S.O.S. Mathematics (http://www.sosmath.com) and The Math Forum@Drexel (http://www.mathforum.org).

EMPLOYERS

Math teachers are needed at middle, junior high, and high schools, including parochial schools, juvenile detention centers, vocational schools, and technical schools. Some Montessori schools are also expanding to include more advanced courses. Though rural areas maintain some schools, most institutions are in towns and cities. Teachers can also find opportunities in "charter" schools, which are smaller, deregulated schools that receive public funding.

STARTING OUT

After completing the teacher certification process, including your months of student teaching, you should work with your college's career services office to find a full-time position. In some states, the departments of education maintain listings of job openings. In addition, many schools advertise teaching positions in the classified sections of the state's major newspapers. You may also directly contact principals and superintendents of the schools in which you would like to work. While waiting for full-time work, you can work as a substitute teacher. Substituting will give you more than a paycheck; you will gain worthwhile teaching experience and learn about different school systems as a sub. In some school districts, you may be able to substitute full time.

ADVANCEMENT

Most math teachers advance in the sense that they become more expert in the job that they have chosen. There is usually an increase in salary as teachers acquire years of experience. Additional training or study can also bring an increase in salary.

Teachers with administrative ability and an interest in administrative work may advance to the position of principal. Others work into supervisory positions or as assistants, helping teachers find appropriate instructional materials and develop certain phases of their courses of study. Teachers may decide to focus their careers more on education than on the subject they teach by moving into teacher education at a college or university. For most of these positions, a master's degree in education is required. Some teachers also make lateral moves into other education-related positions such as school counselor or resource room teacher.

EARNINGS

Most teachers are contracted to work nine months out of the year, though some contracts are made for a full 12 months. When regular school is not in session, teachers are usually expected to conduct summer teaching, planning, or other school-related work.

According to the U.S. Department of Labor, the median annual salary for secondary school teachers was $47,740 in 2006. The lowest 10 percent earned less than $31,760, and the highest 10 percent made $76,100 or more annually. The median annual salary of middle school teachers was $46,300 in 2006. The lowest paid 10 percent of these teachers earned less than $31,450, and the top 10 percent made $73,350 or more per year. The American Federation of Teachers reports that the national average salary for public elementary and secondary school teachers in 2003–04 was $46,597. Teachers can also supplement their earnings by teaching summer classes, coaching sports, sponsoring a club, or doing other extracurricular work. Unions such as the American Federation of Teachers and the National Education Association negotiate with schools over contract conditions such as wages, hours, and benefits. Depending on the state, teachers usually receive a retirement plan, sick leave, and health and life insurance. Some systems grant teachers sabbatical leave.

WORK ENVIRONMENT

Although the job of the math teacher is not physically strenuous, it can be tiring and trying. Teachers must stand for many hours each day, do a lot of talking, show energy and enthusiasm, and handle discipline problems. Despite these often trying tasks, they also have the reward of guiding students in the making of decisions about their lives and futures.

Math teachers work under generally pleasant conditions, though some older schools may have poor heating and electrical systems. Though violence in schools has decreased in recent years, media coverage of the violence has increased along with student fears. In most schools, students are prepared to learn and to perform the work that's required of them. But in some schools, students may be dealing with gangs, drugs, poverty, and other problems, so the environment can be tense and emotional.

School hours are generally 8:00 A.M. to 3:00 P.M., but teachers work more than 40 hours a week. Outside the classroom, they spend a lot of time preparing for classes, grading papers, and directing extracurricular activities. Some work evenings and weekends, coaching school teams or tutoring students. Many teachers enroll in master's or doctoral programs and take evening and summer courses to continue their education.

OUTLOOK

Employment for teachers is predicted to grow at an average rate through 2016, according to the U.S. Department of Labor. Many schools are in short supply of educators, partly due to the large number of teachers expected to retire. As a result, school systems are competing for teachers in many locations, using bonuses and higher pay to lure the most qualified.

The U.S. Department of Education predicts that 336,000 more elementary, middle, and secondary teachers will be needed by 2016 to meet rising enrollments and to replace the large number of retiring teachers. Math teachers, in particular, are in short supply, especially in large cities. The National Education Association believes this will be a challenge because of the low salaries that are paid to secondary school teachers. Higher salaries will be necessary to attract new teachers and retain experienced ones, along with other changes such as smaller classroom sizes and safer schools. Other challenges for the profession involve attracting more men into teaching. The percentage of male teachers at this level continues to decline.

FOR MORE INFORMATION

For information about careers and current issues affecting teachers, contact

American Federation of Teachers
555 New Jersey Avenue, NW
Washington, DC 20001-2029

Tel: 202-879-4400
Email: online@aft.org
http://www.aft.org

For information on student competitions, contact
Mathematical Association of America
1529 Eighteenth Street, NW
Washington, DC 20036-1358
Tel: Tel: 202-387-5200
http://www.maa.org

For information on certification, contact
National Board for Professional Teaching Standards
1525 Wilson Boulevard, Suite 500
Arlington, VA 22209-2451
Tel: 800-228-3224
Email: info@nbpts.org
http://www.nbpts.org

For information on accredited teacher education programs, contact
National Council for Accreditation of Teacher Education
2010 Massachusetts Avenue, NW, Suite 500
Washington, DC 20036-1023
Tel: 202-466-7496
Email: ncate@ncate.org
http://www.ncate.org

For information on teaching careers in mathematics, contact
National Council of Teachers of Mathematics
1906 Association Drive
Reston, VA 20191-1502
Tel: 703-620-9840
http://www.nctm.org

For information on public education, contact
National Education Association
1201 16th Street, NW
Washington, DC 20036-3290
Tel: 202-833-4000
http://www.nea.org

Naturalists

OVERVIEW

The primary role of *naturalists* is to educate the public about the environment and maintain the natural environment on land specifically dedicated to wilderness populations. Their primary responsibilities are preserving, restoring, maintaining, and protecting a natural habitat. Among the related responsibilities in these jobs are teaching, public speaking, writing, giving scientific and ecological demonstrations, and handling public relations and administrative tasks. Naturalists may work in a variety of environments, including private nature centers; local, state, and national parks and forests; wildlife museums; and independent nonprofit conservation and restoration associations. Some of the many job titles a naturalist might hold are wildlife manager, fish and game warden, fish and wildlife officer, land steward, wildlife biologist, and environmental interpreter. Natural resource managers, wildlife conservationists, and ecologists sometimes perform the work of naturalists.

HISTORY

Prior to the 17th century, there was little support for environmental preservation. Instead, wilderness was commonly seen as a vast resource to be controlled. This view began to change during the early years of the industrial revolution, when new energy resources were utilized, establishing an increasing need for petroleum, coal, natural gas, wood, and water for hydropowered energy. In England and France, for example, the rapid depletion of natural forests caused by the increased use of timber for powering the new industries led to demands for forest conservation.

The United States, especially during the 19th century, saw many of its great forests razed, huge tracts of land leveled for open-pit mining and quarrying, and increased disease with the rise of air pollution from the smokestacks of factories, home chimneys, and engine exhaust. Much of the land damage occurred at the same time as a dramatic depletion of wildlife, including elk, antelope, deer, bison, and other animals of the Great Plains. Some types of bear, cougar, and wolf became extinct, as did several kinds of birds, such as the passenger pigeon. In the latter half of the 19th century, the U.S. government set up a commission to develop scientific management of fisheries, established the first national park (Yellowstone National Park in Wyoming, Idaho, and Montana), and set aside the first forest reserves. The modern conservation movement grew out of these early steps.

States also established parks and forests for wilderness conservation. Parks and forests became places where people, especially urban dwellers, could acquaint themselves with the natural settings of their ancestors. Naturalists, employed by the government, institutions of higher education, and various private concerns, were involved not only in preserving and exploring the natural reserves but also in educating the public about the remaining wilderness.

Controversy over the proper role of U.S. parks and forests began soon after their creation (and continues to this day), as the value of these natural areas for logging, recreation, and other human activities conflicted with the ecological need for preservation. President Theodore Roosevelt, a strong supporter of the conservation movement, believed nevertheless in limited industrial projects, such as dams, within the wilderness areas. Despite these controversies, the system of national parks and forests expanded throughout the 20th century. Today, the Agriculture and Interior Departments, and, to a lesser extent, the Department of Defense, have conservation responsibilities for soil, forests, grasslands, water, wildlife, and federally owned land.

In the 1960s and early 1970s, the hazards posed by pollution to both humans and the environment highlighted the importance of nature preservation and public education. Federal agencies were established, such as the Environmental Protection Agency, the Council on Environmental Quality, and the National Oceanic and Atmospheric Administration. Crucial legislation was passed, including the Wilderness Act (1964) and the Endangered Species Act (1969). Naturalists have been closely involved with these conservation efforts and others, shouldering the responsibility to communicate to the public the importance of maintaining diverse ecosystems and to help restore or balance ecosystems under threat.

THE JOB

Because of the impact of human populations on the environment, virtually no area in the United States is truly wild. Land and the animal populations require human intervention to help battle against the human encroachment that is damaging or hindering wildlife. Naturalists work to help wildlife maintain or improve their hold in the world.

The work can be directly involved in maintaining individual populations of animals or plants, overseeing whole ecosystems, or promoting the work of those who are directly involved in the maintenance of the ecosystem. *Fish and wildlife officers* (or *fish and game wardens*) work to preserve and restore the animal populations, including migratory birds that may only be part of the environment temporarily. *Wildlife managers* and *range conservationists* oversee the combination of plants and animals in their territories.

Fish and wildlife officers and wardens study, assist, and help regulate the populations of fish, hunted animals, and protected animals throughout the United States. They may work directly in the parks and reserves, or they may oversee a region within a particular state, even if there are no park lands there. Fish and game wardens control the hunting and fishing of wild populations to make sure that the populations are not overharvested during a season. They monitor the populations of each species off season as well as make sure the species is thriving but is not overpopulating and running the risk of starvation or territory damage. Most people hear about the fish and game wardens when a population of animals has overgrown its territory and needs either to be culled (selectively hunted) or moved. Usually this occurs with the deer population, but it can also apply to predator animals such as the coyote or fox, or scavenger animals such as the raccoon. Because the practice of culling animal populations arouses controversy, the local press usually gives wide coverage to such situations.

The other common time to hear about wildlife wardens is when poaching is uncovered locally. Poaching can be hunting or fishing an animal out of season or hunting or fishing a protected animal. Although we think of poachers in the African plains hunting lions and elephants, poaching is common in the United States for animals such as mountain lions, brown bears, eagles, and wolves. Game wardens target and arrest poachers; punishment can include prison sentences and steep fines.

Wildlife managers, *range managers,* and *conservationists* work to maintain the plant and animal life in a given area. Wildlife managers can work in small local parks or enormous national parks. Range managers work on ranges that have a combination of domestic live-stock and wild population. The U.S. government has leased and per-mitted farmers to graze and raise livestock on federally held ranges, although this program is under increasing attack by environmental-ists. Range managers must ensure that both the domestic and wild populations are living side by side successfully. They make sure that the population of predatory wild animals does not increase enough to deplete the livestock and that the livestock does not overgraze the land and eliminate essential food for the wild animals. Range man-agers and conservationists must test soil and water for nutrients and pollution, count plant and animal populations in every season, and keep in contact with farmers using the land for reports of attacks on livestock or the presence of disease.

Wildlife managers also balance the needs of the humans using or traveling through the land they supervise with those of the animals that live in or travel through that same land. They keep track of the populations of animals and plants and provide food and water when it is lacking naturally. This may involve airdrops of hay and grain during winter months to deer, moose, or elk populations in remote reaches of a national forest, or digging and filling a water reservoir for animals during a drought.

Naturalists in all these positions often have administrative duties such as supervising staff members and volunteers, raising funds (par-ticularly for independent nonprofit organizations), writing grant applications, taking and keeping records and statistics, and main-taining public relations. They may write articles for local or national publications to inform and educate the public about their location or a specific project. They may be interviewed by journalists for reports concerning their site or their work.

Nature walks are often given to groups as a way of educating peo-ple about the land and the work that goes into revitalizing and main-taining it. Tourists, schoolchildren, amateur conservationists and naturalists, social clubs, and retirees commonly attend these walks. On a nature walk, the naturalist may point out specific plants and animals, identify rocks, and discuss soil composition or the natural history of the area (including special environmental strengths and problems). The naturalist may even discuss the indigenous people of the area, especially in terms of how they adapted to the unique aspects of their particular environment. Because such a variety of topics may be brought up, the naturalist must be an environmental generalist, familiar with such subjects as biology, botany, geology, geography, meteorology, anthropology, and history.

Demonstrations, exhibits, and classes are ways that the naturalist can educate the public about the environment. For example, to help

A naturalist at a public aquarium explains a hands-on exhibit to a group of young people. (*Jeff Greenberg, The Image Works*)

children understand oil spills, the naturalist may set up a simple demonstration showing that oil and water do not mix. Sometimes the natural setting already provides an exhibit for the naturalist. Dead fish, birds, and other animals found in a park may help demonstrate the natural life cycle and the process of decomposition. Instruction may also be given on outdoor activities, such as hiking and camping.

For some naturalists, preparing educational materials is a large part of their job. Brochures, fact sheets, pamphlets, and newsletters may be written for people visiting the park or nature center. Materials might also be sent to area residents in an effort to gain public support.

One aspect of protecting any natural area involves communicating facts and debunking myths about how to respect the area and the flora and fauna that inhabit it. Another aspect involves tending managed areas to promote a diversity of plants and animals. This may mean introducing trails and footpaths that provide easy yet noninvasive access for the public; it may mean cordoning off an area to prevent foot traffic from ruining a patch of rare moss; or it may mean instigating a letter-writing campaign to drum up support for legislation to protect a specific area, plant, or animal. It may be easy to get support for protecting the snowshoe rabbit; it is harder to make the public understand the need to preserve and maintain a cave in which bats live.

Some naturalists, such as *directors of nature centers or conservation organizations,* have massive administrative responsibilities. They might recruit volunteers and supervise staff, organize long- and short-term program goals, and handle record-keeping and the budget. To raise money, naturalists may need to speak publicly on a regular basis, write grant proposals, and organize and attend scheduled fund-raising activities and community meetings. Naturalists also try to increase public awareness and support by writing press releases and organizing public workshops, conferences, seminars, meetings, and hearings. In general, naturalists must be available as resources for educating and advising the community.

REQUIREMENTS

High School

If you are interested in this field, you should take a number of basic science courses, including biology, chemistry, and Earth science. Botany courses and clubs are helpful, since they provide direct experience monitoring plant growth and health. Animal care experience, usually obtained through volunteer work, is also helpful. Take English courses in high school to improve your writing skills, which you will use when writing grant proposals and conducting research.

Postsecondary Training

An undergraduate degree in environmental, physical, or natural sciences is generally the minimum educational requirement for becoming a naturalist. Common college majors are biology, forestry, wildlife management, natural resource and park management, natural resources, botany, zoology, chemistry, natural history, and environmental science. Course work in economics, history, anthropology, English, international studies, and communication arts are also helpful.

Graduate education is increasingly required for employment as a naturalist, particularly for upper-level positions. A master's degree in natural science or natural resources is the minimum requirement for supervisory or administrative roles in many of the nonprofit agencies, and several positions require either a doctorate or several years of experience in the field. For positions in agencies with international sites, work abroad is necessary and can be obtained through volunteer positions such as those with the Peace Corps or in paid positions assisting in site administration and management.

Other Requirements

If you are considering a career in this field, you should like working outdoors, as most naturalists spend the majority of their time outside in all kinds of weather. However, along with the desire to work in and with the natural world, you need to be capable of communicating with the human world as well. Excellent writing skills are helpful in preparing educational materials and grant proposals.

Seemingly unrelated skills in this field, such as engine repair and basic carpentry, can be essential to managing a post. Because of the remote locations of many of the work sites, self-sufficiency in operating and maintaining the equipment allows the staff to lose fewer days because of equipment breakdown.

EXPLORING

One of the best ways to learn about the job of a naturalist is to volunteer at one of the many national and state parks or nature centers. These institutions often recruit volunteers for outdoor work. College students, for example, are sometimes hired to work as summer or part-time nature guides. Outdoor recreation and training organizations, such as Outward Bound (http://www.outwardbound.org) and the National Outdoor Leadership School (http://www.nols.edu), are especially good resources. Most volunteer positions, though, require a high school diploma and some college credit.

You should also consider college internship programs. In addition, conservation programs and organizations throughout the country and the world offer opportunities for volunteer work in a wide variety of areas, including working with the public, giving lectures and guided tours, and working with others to build or maintain an ecosystem. For more frequent, up-to-date information, you can read newsletters, such as *Environmental Career Opportunities* (http://ecojobs.com), that post internship and job positions. The Web site, Environmental Career.com (http://environmental-jobs.com) also offers job listings.

Read books and magazines about nature and the career of naturalists. One interesting publication is *The American Naturalist,* published by the University of Chicago Press for the American Society of Naturalists. Visit http://www.journals.uchicago.edu/AN/home.html to read sample articles.

EMPLOYERS

Naturalists may be employed by state agencies such as departments of wildlife, fish and game, or natural resources. They may work at the federal level for the U.S. Fish and Wildlife Service or the National Park Service. Naturalists may also work in the private sector for such employers as nature centers, arboretums, and botanical gardens.

STARTING OUT

If you hope to become a park employee, the usual method of entry is through part-time or seasonal employment for the first several jobs, then a full-time position. Because it is difficult to get experience before completing a college degree, and because seasonal employment is common, you should prepare to seek supplemental income for your first few years in the field.

International experience is helpful with agencies that work beyond the U.S. borders. This can be through the Peace Corps or other volunteer organizations that work with local populations on land and habitat management or restoration. Other volunteer experience is available through local restoration programs on sites in your area. Organizations such as the Nature Conservancy (http://nature.org), The Trust for Public Land (http://www.tpl.org), and many others buy land to restore, and these organizations rely extensively on volunteer labor for stewarding and working the land. Rescue and release centers work with injured and abandoned wildlife to rehabilitate them. Opportunities at these centers can include banding wild animals for tracking, working with injured or adolescent animals for release training, and adapting unreleasable animals to educational programs and presentations.

ADVANCEMENT

In some settings, such as small nature centers, there may be little room for advancement. In larger organizations, experience and additional education can lead to increased responsibility and pay. Among the higher-level positions is that of director, handling supervisory, administrative, and public relations tasks.

Advancement into upper-level management and supervisory positions usually requires a graduate degree, although people with a graduate degree and no work experience will still have to start in nearly entry-level positions. So you can either work a few years and then return to school to get an advanced degree or complete your education and start in the same position you would have without the degree. The advanced degree will allow you eventually to move further up in the organizational structure.

EARNINGS

Earnings for naturalists are influenced by several factors, including the naturalist's specific job (for example, a wildlife biologist, a water and soil conservationist, or a game manager), the employer (for example, a state or federal agency), and the naturalist's experience and education. The U.S. Fish and Wildlife Service reports that biologists working for this department have starting salaries at the GS-5 to GS-7 levels. In 2008, biologists at the GS-5 pay level earned annual salaries that ranged from $26,264 to $34,139, and those at the GS-7 level earned annual salaries that ranged from $32,534 to $42,290. The U.S. Fish and Wildlife Service further reports that biologists can expect to advance to GS-11 or GS-12 levels. In 2008, basic yearly pay at these levels was $48,148 and $57,709, respectively. In general, those working for state agencies have somewhat lower earnings, particularly at the entry level. And, again, the specific job a naturalist performs affects earnings. For example, the U.S. Department of Labor reports that conservation scientists had a median annual salary of $54,970 in 2006. However, some conservation workers put in 40-hour weeks and make less than $20,000 annually. As with other fields, management positions are among the highest paying. Salaries for managers may range from $45,000 to $75,000 or more annually. Keep in mind, though, that this position and these earnings are at the top of the field. The candidate who meets the qualifications for this position would have extensive experience and be responsible for, among other things, managing research programs statewide, hiring lower-level managers, prioritizing and directing research, and acting as the department representative to other government agencies and public groups.

For some positions, housing and vehicles may be provided. Other benefits, depending on employer, may include health insurance, vacation time, and retirement plans.

WORK ENVIRONMENT

Field naturalists spend a majority of their working hours outdoors. Depending on the location, the naturalist must work in a wide variety of weather conditions: from frigid cold to sweltering heat to torrential rain. Remote sites are common, and long periods of working either in isolation or in small teams is not uncommon for field research and management. Heavy lifting, hauling, working with machinery and hand tools, digging, planting, harvesting, and tracking may fall to the naturalist working in the field. One wildlife manager in Montana spent every daylight hour for several days in a row literally running up and down snow-covered mountains, attempting to tranquilize and collar a mountain lion. Clearly, this can be a physically demanding job.

Indoor work includes scheduling, planning, and classroom teaching. Data gathering and maintaining logs and records are required for many jobs. Naturalists may need to attend and speak at local community meetings. They may have to read detailed legislative bills to analyze the impact of legislation before it becomes law.

Those in supervisory positions, such as directors, are often so busy with administrative and organizational tasks that they may spend little of their workday outdoors. Work that includes guided tours and walks through nature areas is frequently seasonal and usually dependent on daily visitors.

Full-time naturalists usually work about 35 to 40 hours per week. Overtime is often required, and for those naturalists working in areas visited by campers, camping season is extremely busy and can require much overtime. Wildlife and range managers may be on call during storms and severe weather. Seasonal work, such as burn season for land managers and stewards, may require overtime and frequent weekend work.

Naturalists have special occupational hazards, such as working with helicopters, small airplanes, all-terrain vehicles, and other modes of transport through rugged landscapes and into remote regions. Adverse weather conditions and working in rough terrain make illness and injury more likely. Naturalists must be able to get along with the variety of people using the area and may encounter armed individuals who are poaching or otherwise violating the law.

Naturalists also have a number of unique benefits. Most prominent is the chance to live and work in some of the most beautiful places in the world. For many individuals, the lower salaries are offset by the recreational and lifestyle opportunities afforded by living and working in such scenic areas. In general, occupational stress is low, and most naturalists appreciate the opportunity to continually learn about and work to improve the environment.

OUTLOOK

The employment outlook for naturalists is expected to be fair in the next decade. While a growing public concern about environmental issues may cause an increased demand for naturalists, this trend could be offset by government cutbacks in funding for nature programs. Reduced government spending on education may indirectly affect the demand for naturalists, as school districts would have less money to spend on outdoor education and recreation. Despite the limited number of available positions, the number of well-qualified applicants is expected to remain high.

FOR MORE INFORMATION

For information on careers, contact
American Society of Naturalists
http://www.amnat.org

For information on environmental expeditions, contact
Earthwatch Institute
3 Clock Tower Place, Suite 100
PO Box 75
Maynard, MA 01754-0075
Tel: 800-776-0188
Email: info@earthwatch.org
http://www.earthwatch.org

For information about career opportunities, contact
Bureau of Land Management
U.S. Department of the Interior
1849 C Street, Room 406-LS
Washington, DC 20240-0001

This group offers internships and fellowships for college and graduate students with an interest in environmental issues. For information, contact
Friends of the Earth
1717 Massachusetts Avenue, NW, 600
Washington, DC 20036-2002
Tel: 877-843-8687
Email: foe@foe.org
http://www.foe.org

For information on a variety of conservation programs, contact
National Wildlife Federation
11100 Wildlife Center Drive
Reston, VA 20190-5362
Tel: 800-822-9919
http://www.nwf.org

For information on volunteer opportunities, contact
Student Conservation Association
PO Box 550
Charlestown, NC 03603-0550
Tel: 603-543-1700
http://www.sca-inc.org

For information on careers, contact
U.S. Fish and Wildlife Service
U.S. Department of the Interior
Division of Human Resources
4401 North Fairfax Drive, Mailstop: 2000
Arlington, VA 22203-1610
http://hr.fws.gov/HR/Careers_FWS.htm

For information on federal employment, contact
USAJOBS
Office of Personnel Management
http://www.usajobs.opm.gov

Nursing Instructors

QUICK FACTS

School Subjects
Biology
Chemistry
Health

Personal Skills
Helping/teaching
Technical/scientific

Work Environment
Primarily indoors
Primarily multiple locations

Minimum Education Level
Bachelor's degree

Salary Range
$24,942 to $55,280 to
$184,241

Certification or Licensing
Required

Outlook
Much faster than the average

DOT
075

GOE
12.03.02

NOC
N/A

O*NET-SOC
25-1072.00

OVERVIEW

Nursing instructors teach patient care to nursing students in classroom and clinical settings. They demonstrate care methods and monitor hands-on learning by their students. They instruct students in the principles and applications of biological and psychological subjects related to nursing. Some nursing instructors specialize in teaching specific areas of nursing such as surgical or oncological nursing.

Nursing instructors may be full professors, assistant professors, instructors, or lecturers, depending on their education and the facilities' nursing programs. There are approximately 39,000 nursing instructors employed in the United States.

HISTORY

In 1873, the first school of nursing in the United States was founded in Boston. In 1938, New York state passed the first law requiring that practical nurses be licensed. Even though the first school for the training of practical nurses had started almost 65 years before, and the establishment of other schools followed, the training programs lacked uniformity.

Shortly after licensure requirements surfaced, a movement toward organized training programs began that would help to ensure quality standards in the field. The role and training of nurses have undergone radical changes since the first nursing schools were opened. Education standards for nurses have been improving constantly since that time. Nurses are now required by all states to be appropriately educated and licensed to practice. Extended programs of training are offered throughout the country. The field of nursing serves an important role as a part of the health care system.

According to the American Association of Colleges of Nursing (AACN), the field of nursing is the nation's largest health care profession, and nursing students account for more than half of all health profession students in the United States. The U.S. Department of Labor reports there are approximately 2.5 million registered nurses (RNs) nationwide. This workforce, however, is aging, and the department notes that thousands of RNs will be needed through the first decades of the 21st century simply to replace those nurses who leave the profession.

The AACN reports that nearly 43,000 qualified applicants to baccalaureate nursing programs were not accepted in 2006. Nearly 71 percent of responding schools said that an insufficient number of faculty was a factor for not accepting all applicants. As more students apply to nursing school, more nursing instructors will be needed to teach students and make up for staffing shortages.

Several factors are contributing to the shortage of nursing faculty. Bachelor's degree nursing programs have had difficulty in attracting qualified faculty. Budgetary limitations, competition with clinical service agencies, and lack of qualified nursing instructors have reduced the number of quality instructors. A lack of classroom space and clinical training sites—highly sought after due to the emphasis on community-based services—also limit the number of nursing educators.

THE JOB

Nursing instructors teach in colleges and universities or nursing schools. They teach in classrooms and in clinical settings. Their duties depend on the facility, the nursing program, and the instructor's education level. Some nursing instructors specialize in specific subjects such as chemistry or anatomy, or in a type of nursing activity, such as pediatric nursing.

Many health care facilities partner with area nursing programs, so the students can actually practice what they are learning under the supervision of nursing staff and instructors. For example, the students may spend time in a hospital environment learning pediatrics and surgical care and additional time in a nursing home setting learning the health care needs of the elderly and disabled. Classroom instruction and clinical training depend on the nursing program and the degree conferred.

Mary Bell, RN, who has 12 years of nursing experience, taught classes part time as an associate professor in Indiana. Classroom teaching and clinical practice were her responsibilities.

Bell says, "As part of the clinical instruction, students conferred with me regarding the patients. They assessed the patients and learned how to chart information and statistics. Sometimes their patient observations were very keen.

"I loved the clinical part of teaching," she says. "The students often brought a new perspective to nursing. They were always eager to learn and to share what they learned.

"Nursing technology and care is always changing, and the instructor shouldn't mind being challenged," states Bell. She goes on to say that the instructor must be able to create dialogue so there is an exchange of information and ideas. "It is a process between student and teacher," she observes.

Nursing instructors must spend a lot of preparation time outside the classroom and clinical setting, according to Bell. For example, the instructor must work with head nurses or charge nurses to determine the students' patient assignments. They must review patients' charts and be well informed about their current conditions prior to the student nurses appearing for their clinical instruction. Plus, there are the usual teaching responsibilities such as course planning, paper grading, and test preparation. Involvement often extends beyond the classroom.

"Professors at universities and colleges are expected to be involved with the community," says Bell. They may be required to speak to community groups or consult with businesses, and they are encouraged to be active in professional associations and on academic committees.

"In addition, many larger institutions expect professors to do research and be published in nursing or medical journals," Bell notes.

Teaching load and research requirements vary by institution and program. Full professors usually spend more of their time conducting research and publishing than assistant professors, instructors, and lecturers.

Often nursing instructors actively work in the nursing field along with teaching. "They will do this to maintain current hands-on experience and to advance their careers," Bell acknowledges. "It is a huge commitment. But," she adds, "it's great being able to see the light bulb turn on in the students' heads."

REQUIREMENTS
High School
If you are interested in becoming a nursing instructor, take classes in health and the sciences to prepare for a medical career. Since nurs-

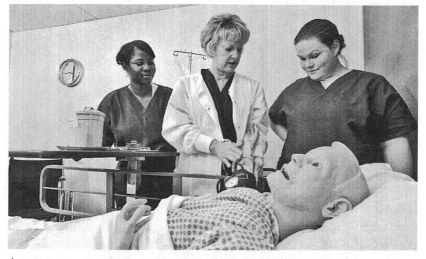

A nursing instructor supervises students as they practice
nursing techniques on a dummy that simulates an elderly patient.
(Bob Daemmrich, The Image Works)

ing instructors begin as nurses themselves, you need to take classes
that will prepare you for nursing programs. Talk to your guidance
counselor about course requirements for specific programs, but plan
on taking biology, chemistry, mathematics, and English courses to
help build the strong foundation necessary for nursing school.

Postsecondary Training

Most nursing instructors first work as registered nurses and, therefore, have completed either a two-year associate's degree program,
a three-year diploma program, or a four-year bachelor's degree program in nursing. Which of the three training programs to choose
depends on your career goals. As a nurse, you should also have considerable clinical nursing experience before considering teaching.

Most universities and colleges require that their full-time professors have doctoral degrees, but many hire master's degree holders for
part-time and temporary teaching positions. Two-year colleges may
hire full-time teachers who have master's degrees. Smaller institutions or nursing schools may hire part-time nursing instructors who
have a bachelor's degree.

Certification or Licensing

In order to practice as a registered nurse, you first must become
licensed in the state in which you plan to work. Licensed RNs must
graduate from an accredited school of nursing and pass a national
examination. In order to renew their license, RNs must show proof

of continued education and pass renewal exams. Most states honor licenses granted in other states, as long as scores are acceptable.

Other Requirements

In order to succeed as a nursing instructor, you must enjoy teaching and nursing. You should have excellent organizational and leadership skills and be able to communicate well with professional staff and students of all ages. You should be able to demonstrate skilled nursing techniques. Since you will be responsible for all the care your students administer to patients, you must have good supervision skills. In addition, you should be able to teach your students the humane side of nursing that is so important in dealing with patients. New medical technologies, patient treatments, and medications are constantly being developed, so nursing instructors must stay abreast of new information in the medical field. They need to be up to date on the use of new medical equipment that is used for patient care.

EXPLORING

While in high school, you can explore your interest in the nursing field in a number of ways. Consult your high school guidance counselor, school nurse, and local community nurses for information. A visit to a hospital or nursing clinic can give you a chance to observe the roles and duties of nurses in the facility and may give you the opportunity to talk one-on-one with staff members. Check to see if you can volunteer to work in a hospital, nursing home, or clinic after school, on weekends, or during summer vacation to further explore your interest.

To get a better sense of the teaching work involved in being a nursing instructor, explore your interest and talents as a teacher. Spend some time with one of your teachers after school, and ask to look at lecture notes and record-keeping procedures. Ask your teacher about the amount of work that goes into preparing a class or directing an extracurricular activity. To get some firsthand teaching experience, volunteer for a peer tutoring program. Visit NursingNet (http://www.nursingnet.org), Nursing World (http://www.nursingworld.org), DiscoverNursing (http://www.discovernursing.com), and other nursing-related Web sites to keep up to date in this field.

EMPLOYERS

Approximately 39,000 nursing instructors are employed in the United States. Nursing instructors work in hospitals, clinics, colleges, and universities that offer nursing education programs. Instructors' jobs can vary greatly, depending on the employer. Many nursing instruc-

Nursing Specialties

In addition to training students to become traditional nurses, nursing instructors also teach a variety of specialized nursing disciplines. Here are just a few of the nursing specialties taught by nursing instructors:

- Anesthesia
- Clinical Care
- Critical Care
- Dermatology
- Emergency Room
- Forensic Science
- Geriatric Care
- Hospice Care
- Midwifery
- Neonatal
- Nurse Practitioner
- Occupational Health
- Oncology
- Psychiatric
- Public Health
- Surgical

tors associated with hospitals or medical clinics work in the nursing field in addition to teaching. Those employed by large universities and colleges are more focused on academia, conducting medical research, and writing medical reports of their findings.

STARTING OUT

Because you should first obtain practical experience in this field, begin by becoming a registered nurse. After graduating from an approved nursing program and passing licensure examinations, you can apply directly to hospitals, nursing homes, companies, and government agencies for employment. Jobs can also be obtained through school career services offices, employment agencies specializing in placement of nursing personnel, or through states' employment offices. Other sources of jobs include nurses' associations, professional journals, and newspaper want ads.

ADVANCEMENT

In hospitals and clinics, nursing instructors generally advance by moving up in staff ranks. Positions with higher levels of authority, and hence, higher pay, include clinical nurse specialists, advanced practice nurses, nurse supervisors, or medical administrators.

Those who work in nursing schools, colleges, or universities may advance through the academic ranks from a part-time adjunct to a full-time instructor to assistant professor to associate professor, and finally to full professor. From there, those interested in administration may become deans or directors of nursing programs. As professors advance in their careers, they frequently spend less time in the classroom and more time conducting research, public speaking, and writing.

EARNINGS

Educational background, experience, responsibilities, geographic location, and the hiring institution are factors influencing the earnings of nursing instructors.

According to the U.S. Department of Labor, nursing instructors and teachers had median annual earnings of $55,280 in 2006. Ten percent earned less than $34,140 annually, and 10 percent earned more than $88,640 annually. The American Association of Colleges of Nursing's report *2002–2003 Salaries of Instructional and Administrative Nursing Faculty in Baccalaureate and Graduate Programs in Nursing* shows a wide range of earnings based on the type of institution an instructor works at, the instructor's level of education, and position held. The reported low of $24,942 was for an instructor without a doctorate who worked at a public school. The reported high, $184,241, was for a full professor with a doctorate who worked at a private school. These earnings, however, are at extreme ends of the pay scales. By rank, nursing teachers with doctoral degrees had the following averages for the 2002–03 academic year: instructor, $48,084; assistant professor, $54,128; associate professor, $63,172; and full professor, $77,590.

Full-time faculty typically receive such benefits as health insurance, retirement plans, paid sick leave, and, in some cases, funds for work-related expenses such as educational conferences.

WORK ENVIRONMENT

Nursing instructors work in colleges, universities, or nursing schools. Their clinical instruction can take place in any number of health care facilities including doctors' offices, medical clinics, hospitals, institutions, and nursing homes. Most health care environments are clean and well lighted. Inner-city facilities may be in less than desirable locations, and safety may be an issue.

All health-related careers have some health and disease risks; however, adherence to health and safety guidelines greatly minimizes the chance of contracting infectious diseases such as hepatitis and AIDS. Medical knowledge and good safety measures are also needed to limit exposure to toxic chemicals, radiation, and other hazards.

OUTLOOK

The U.S. Department of Labor predicts that employment for registered nurses will grow much faster than the average for all occupations through 2016. In addition, those practicing nursing specialties will also be in great demand. Because of this, there will be a corresponding demand for nursing instructors. There is an ongoing shortage of nursing instructors due to a declining interest by nurses in pursuing careers as educators. Nursing educators earn much lower salaries than those paid to nurses in clinical settings, which has reduced interest in the field. Additionally, the average age of doctorally prepared nursing professors was 56.6 years in 2002–03, according to the American Association of Colleges of Nursing. This means that during the next decade a large percentage of nursing school professors will retire. Their replacements, naturally, are drawn from the instructor ranks, and this should also add to a shortage of and demand for nursing teachers.

FOR MORE INFORMATION

For more information on becoming a nursing instructor, contact the following organizations:

American Association of Colleges of Nursing
One Dupont Circle, NW, Suite 530
Washington, DC 20036-1135
Tel: 202-463-6930
http://www.aacn.nche.edu

American Nurses Association
8515 Georgia Avenue, Suite 400
Silver Spring, MD 20910-3492
Tel: 800-274-4262
http://www.nursingworld.org

Park Rangers

OVERVIEW

Park rangers enforce laws and regulations in national, state, and county parks. They help care for and maintain parks as well as inform, guide, and ensure the safety of park visitors.

HISTORY

Congress started the National Park System in the United States in 1872 when Yellowstone National Park was created. The National Park Service (NPS), a bureau of the U.S. Department of the Interior, was created in 1916 to preserve, protect, and manage the national, cultural, historical, and recreational areas of the National Park System. At that time, the park system contained less than 1 million acres. Today, the country's national parks cover more than 84 million acres of mountains, plains, deserts, swamps, historic sites, lakeshores, forests, rivers, battlefields, memorials, archaeological properties, and recreation areas.

All NPS areas are given one of the following designations: National Park, National Historical Park, National Battlefield, National Battlefield Park, National Battlefield Site, National Military Site, National Memorial, National Historic Site, National Monument, National Preserve, National Seashore, National Parkway, National Lakeshore, National Reserve, National River, National Wild and Scenic River, National Recreation Area, or just Park. (The White House in Washington, D.C., for example, which is administered by the NPS, is officially a Park.)

To protect the fragile, irreplaceable resources located in these areas, and to protect the millions of visitors who climb, ski, hike, boat, fish, and otherwise explore them, the National Park Service employs park rangers. State and county parks employ rangers to perform similar tasks.

THE JOB

Park rangers have a wide variety of duties that range from conservation efforts to bookkeeping. Their first responsibility is, however, safety. Rangers who work in parks with treacherous terrain, dangerous wildlife (such as buffalo, grizzly bears, and mountain lions), or severe weather must make sure hikers, campers, and backpackers follow outdoor safety codes. They often require visitors to register at park offices so that rangers will know when someone does not return from a hike or climb and may be hurt. Rangers often participate in search-and-rescue missions for visitors who are lost or injured in parks. In mountainous or forested regions, they may use helicopters or horses for searches.

Rangers also protect parks from inappropriate use and other threats from humans. They register vehicles and collect parking and registration fees, which are used to help maintain roads and facilities. They enforce the laws, regulations, and policies of the parks, patrolling to prevent vandalism, theft, and harm to wildlife. Rangers may arrest and evict people who violate these laws. Some of their efforts to conserve and protect park resources include keeping jeeps and other motorized vehicles off sand dunes and other fragile lands. They make sure visitors do not litter, pollute water, chop down trees for firewood, or start unsafe campfires that could lead to catastrophic forest fires. When forest fires do start, rangers often help with the dangerous task of putting them out.

Park rangers carry out various tasks associated with the management of the natural resources within our National Park System. An important aspect of this responsibility is the care and management of both native and exotic animal species found within the boundaries of the parks. Duties may include conducting basic research, as well as disseminating information about the reintroduction of native animal populations and the protection of the natural habitat that supports the animals.

Rangers also help with conservation, research, and ecology efforts that are not connected to visitors' use of the park. They may study wildlife behavior patterns, for example, by tagging and following certain animals. In this way, they can chart the animals' migration patterns, assess the animals' impact on the park's ecosystem, and determine whether the park should take measures to control or encourage certain wildlife populations.

A park ranger at Shenandoah National Park in Virginia talks with two day hikers. *(Jeff Greenberg, The Image Works)*

Some rangers study plant life and may work with conservationists to reintroduce native or endangered species. They measure the quality of water and air in the park to monitor and mitigate the effects of pollution and other threats from sources outside park boundaries.

In addition, park rangers help visitors enjoy and experience parks. In historical and other cultural parks, such as the Alamo in San Antonio, Independence Hall in Philadelphia, and the Lincoln Home in Springfield, Illinois, rangers give lectures and provide guided tours explaining the history and significance of the site. In natural parks, they may lecture on conservation topics, provide information about plants and animals in the park, and take visitors on interpretive walks, pointing out the area's flora, fauna, and geological characteristics. At a Civil War battlefield park, such as Gettysburg National Military Park in Pennsylvania or Vicksburg National Military Park in Mississippi, they explain to visitors what happened at that site during the Civil War and its implications for our country.

Park rangers are also indispensable to the management and administration of parks. They issue permits to visitors and vehicles and help plan the recreational activities in parks. They help in the planning and managing of park budgets. They keep records and compile statistics concerning weather conditions, resource conservation activities, and the number of park visitors.

Many rangers supervise other workers in the parks who build and maintain park facilities, work part time or seasonally, or operate concession facilities. Rangers often have their own park maintenance responsibilities, such as trail-building, landscaping, and caring for visitor centers.

In some parks, rangers are specialists in certain areas of park protection, safety, or management. For example, in areas with heavy snowfalls and a high incidence of avalanches, experts in avalanche control and snow safety are designated *snow rangers*. They monitor snow conditions and patrol park areas to make sure visitors are not lost in snowslides.

REQUIREMENTS

High School

To prepare for the necessary college course load, you should take courses in earth science, biology, mathematics, English, and speech. Any classes or activities that deal with plant and animal life, the weather, geography, and interacting with others will be helpful.

Postsecondary Training

Employment as a federal or state park ranger requires either a college degree or a specific amount of education and experience. Approximately 200 colleges and universities offer bachelor's degree programs in park management and park recreation. To meet employment requirements, students in other relevant college programs must accumulate at least 24 semester hours of academic credit in park recreation and management, history, behavioral sciences, forestry, botany, geology, or other applicable subject areas.

Without a degree, you will need three years of experience in parks or conservation and you must show an understanding of what is required in park work. In addition, you must demonstrate good communications skills. A combination of education and experience can also fulfill job requirements, with one academic year of study equaling nine months of experience. Also, the orientation and training a ranger receives on the job may be supplemented with formal training courses.

To succeed as a ranger, you will need skills in protecting forests, parks, and wildlife and in interpreting natural or historical resources. Law enforcement and management skills are also important. If you wish to move into management positions, you may need a graduate degree. Approximately 50 universities offer master's degrees in park recreation and management and 16 have doctoral programs.

U.S. Park Facts

- As of 2004, there were 5,842 state park areas comprising more than 13 million acres.
- In 2001, there were 735 million visitors to state parks.
- Slightly more than 91 percent of all visitors to state parks were day-time users.
- Nearly 272,624,000 people visited national parks in 2006.
- The 10 most popular national parks in 2006 (by number of visits) were: 1) Great Smoky Mountains [http://www.nps.gov/grsm]; 2) Grand Canyon [http://www.nps.gov/grca]; 3) Yosemite [http://www.nps.gov/yose]; 4) Yellowstone [http://www.nps.gov/yell]; 5) Olympic [http://www.nps.gov/olym]; 6) Rocky Mountain [http://www.nps.gov/romo]; 7) Zion [http://www.nps.gov/zion]; 8) Cuyahoga Valley [http://www.nps.gov/cuva]; 9) Grand Teton [http://www.nps.gov/grte]; 10) Acadia [http://www.nps.gov/acad].
- The largest national park is Wrangell-St. Elias National Park and Preserve (http://www.nps.gov/wrst). Its size: 13.2 million acres. The smallest: Thaddeus Kosciuszko National Memorial (http://www.nps.gov/thko), which is less than 0.02 acres.

Sources: National Association of State Park Directors, National Park Service

Other Requirements

In order to be a good park ranger, you should believe in the importance of the country's park resources and the mission of the park system. If you enjoy working outdoors, independently and with others, you may enjoy park ranger work. Rangers need self-confidence, patience, and the ability to stay levelheaded during emergencies. To participate in rescues, you need courage, physical stamina, and endurance, and to deal with visitors you must have tact, sincerity, a personable nature, and a sense of humor. A sense of camaraderie among fellow rangers also can add to the enjoyment of being a park ranger.

EXPLORING

If you are interested in exploring park ranger work, you may wish to apply for part-time or seasonal work in national, state, or county parks. Such workers usually perform maintenance and other unskilled tasks, but they have opportunities to observe park rangers and talk with them about their work. You might also choose to work as a volunteer. Many park research activities, study projects, and rehabilitation efforts are conducted by volunteer groups affiliated with universities or conservation organizations, and these activities can provide insight into the work done by park rangers.

EMPLOYERS

Park rangers in the National Park Service are employed by the U.S. Department of the Interior. Other rangers may be employed by other federal agencies or by state and county agencies in charge of their respective parks.

STARTING OUT

Many workers enter national park ranger jobs after working part time or seasonally at different parks. These workers often work at information desks or in fire control or law enforcement positions. Some help maintain trails, collect trash, or perform forestry activities. If you are interested in applying for a park ranger job with the federal government, contact your local Federal Job Information Center or the federal Office of Personnel Management (http://www.usajobs.opm.gov) in Washington, D.C. for application information. To find jobs in state parks, you should write to the appropriate state departments for information.

ADVANCEMENT

Nearly all rangers start in entry-level positions, which means that nearly all higher-level openings are filled by the promotion of current workers. Entry-level rangers may move into positions as district ranger or park manager, or they may become specialists in resource management or park planning. Rangers who show management skills and become park managers may move into administrative positions in the district, regional, or national headquarters.

The orientation and training a ranger receives on the job may be supplemented with formal training courses. Training for job skills unique to the National Park Service is available at the Horace M. Albright Training Center at Grand Canyon National Park in Arizona and the Stephen T. Mather Training Center at Harpers Ferry, West Virginia. In addition, training is available at the Federal Law Enforcement Training Center in Glynco, Georgia.

EARNINGS

Rangers in the National Park Service are usually hired at the GS-5 grade level, with a base salary of $26,264 in 2008. More experienced or educated rangers may enter the Park Service at the GS-9 level, which pays $39,795 to start. The average ranger is generally at about the second step of the GS-7 level, which translated to a salary of $33,618 in 2008. The most experienced rangers can earn $42,290, the highest salary step in the G-7 level.

To move beyond this level, most rangers must become supervisors, subdistrict rangers, district rangers, or division chiefs. At these higher levels, people can earn more than $90,000 per year. These positions are difficult to obtain, however, because the turnover rate for positions above the GS-7 level is exceptionally low. The government may provide housing to rangers who work in remote areas.

Rangers in state parks work for the state government. According to the National Association of State Park Directors, rangers employed by state parks earned average starting salaries of $24,611 in 2004. They receive comparable salaries and benefits, including paid vacations, sick leave, paid holidays, health and life insurance, and pension plans.

WORK ENVIRONMENT

Rangers work in parks all over the country, from the Okefenokee Swamp in Florida to the Rocky Mountains of Colorado. They work in the mountains and forests of Hawaii, Alaska, and California and in urban and suburban parks throughout the United States.

National park rangers are hired to work 40 hours per week, but their actual working hours can be long and irregular, with a great deal of overtime. They may receive extra pay or time off for working overtime. Some rangers are on call 24 hours a day for emergencies. During the peak tourist seasons, rangers work longer hours. Although many rangers work in offices, many also work outside in all kinds of climates and weather, and most work in a combination of the two settings. Workers may be called upon to risk their own health to rescue injured visitors in cold, snow, rain, and darkness. Rangers in Alaska must adapt to long daylight hours in the summer and short daylight hours in the winter. Working outdoors in beautiful surroundings, however, can be wonderfully stimulating and rewarding for the right kind of worker.

OUTLOOK

Park ranger jobs are scarce and competition for them is fierce. The National Park Service has reported that the ratio of applicants to available positions is sometimes as high as 100 to one. As a result, applicants should attain the greatest number and widest variety of applicable skills possible. They may wish to study subjects they can use in other fields: forestry, land management, conservation, wildlife management, history, and natural sciences, for example.

The scarcity of openings is expected to continue indefinitely. Job seekers, therefore, may wish to apply for outdoor work with agencies other than the NPS, including other federal land and resource management agencies and similar state and local agencies. Such agencies usually have more openings.

FOR MORE INFORMATION

For information about state parks and employment opportunities, contact
National Association of State Park Directors
8829 Woodyhill Road
Raleigh, NC 27613-1134
Tel: 919-676-8365
Email: NASPD@nc.rr.com
http://www.naspd.org

For information about careers, job openings, and national parks, contact
National Park Service
1849 C Street, NW
Washington, DC 20240-0001
Tel: 202-208-6843
http://www.nps.gov

For general career information, contact the following organizations:
National Parks Conservation Association
1300 19th Street, NW, Suite 300
Washington, DC 20036-1628
Tel: 800-628-7275
Email: npca@npca.org
http://www.npca.org

National Recreation and Park Association
22377 Belmont Ridge Road
Ashburn, VA 20148-4150
Tel: 703-858-0784
http://www.nrpa.org

For information on volunteer opportunities, contact
Student Conservation Association
689 River Road
PO Box 550
Charlestown, NH 03603-0550
Tel: 603-543-1700
http://www.thesca.org

Preschool Teachers

OVERVIEW

Preschool teachers promote the general education of children under the age of five. They help students develop physically, socially, and emotionally, work with them on language and communications skills, and help cultivate their cognitive abilities. They also work with families to support parents in raising their young children and reinforcing skills at home. They plan and lead activities developed in accordance with the specific ages and needs of the children they teach. It is the goal of all preschool teachers to help students develop the skills, interests, and individual creativity that they will use for the rest of their lives. Many schools and districts consider *kindergarten teachers,* who teach students five years of age, to be preschool teachers. For the purposes of this article, kindergarten teachers will be included in this category. There are approximately 430,000 preschool teachers and 170,000 kindergarten teachers in the United States.

HISTORY

Friedrich Froebel, a German educator, founded the first kindergarten ("child's garden" in German) in 1837 in Blankenburg, Germany. He also taught adults how to be kindergarten teachers. One of his adult students, Mrs. Carl Schurz, moved to the United States and started the first kindergarten of this country in Watertown, Wisconsin, in the mid-1800s. By 1873, St. Louis added the first American public kindergarten, and preschools for students under age five began to spring up in Europe around this same time. Preschools were introduced into the United States in the 1920s.

QUICK FACTS

School Subjects
Art
English
Family and consumer science

Personal Skills
Communication/ideas
Helping/teaching

Work Environment
Primarily indoors
Primarily one location

Minimum Education Level
Some postsecondary training

Salary Range
$14,870 to $22,680 to
  $71,410+

Certification or Licensing
Recommended

Outlook
About as fast as the average

DOT
092

GOE
12.03.03

NOC
4142

O*NET-SOC
25-2011.00, 25-2012.00

Preschool programs expanded rapidly in the United States during the 1960s, due in large part to the government instituting the Head Start program, which was designed to help preschool-aged children from low-income families receive educational and socialization opportunities that would better prepare them for elementary school. This program also allowed the childrens' parents to work during the day. Around the same time, many U.S. public school systems began developing mandatory kindergarten programs for five-year-olds, and today many schools, both preschool and elementary, and both public and private, are offering full-day kindergarten programs.

THE JOB

Preschool teachers plan and lead activities that build on children's abilities and curiosity and aid them in developing skills and characteristics that help them grow. Because children develop at varying skill levels as well as have different temperaments, preschool teachers need to develop a flexible schedule with time allowed for music, art, playtime, academics, rest, and other activities.

Preschool teachers plan activities that encourage children to develop skills appropriate to their developmental needs. For example, they plan activities based on the understanding that a three-year-old child has different motor skills and reasoning abilities than a five-year-old child. They work with the youngest students on learning the days of the week and the recognition of colors, seasons, and animal names and characteristics; they help older students with number and letter recognition and even simple writing skills. Preschool teachers help children with basic, yet important, tasks like tying shoelaces and washing hands before eating. Attention to the individual needs of each child is vital: Preschool teachers need to be aware of these needs and capabilities, and when possible, adapt activities to the specific needs of the individual child. Self-confidence and the development of communication skills are encouraged in preschools. For example, teachers may give children simple art projects, such as finger painting, and have children show and explain their finished projects to the rest of the class. Show and tell, or "sharing time" as it is often called, gives students opportunities to speak and listen to others.

"A lot of what I teach is based on social skills," says June Gannon, a preschool teacher in Amherst, New Hampshire. "During our circle time, we say hello to one another, sing songs, have show and tell, talk about the weather and do calendar events. We then move on to language arts, which may include talking to children about rules, good listening, helping, sharing, etc., using puppets, work papers, games, and songs."

Preschool teachers adopt many parental responsibilities for the children. They greet the children in the morning and supervise them throughout the day. Often these responsibilities can be quite demanding and complicated. In harsh weather, for example, preschool teachers contend not only with boots, hats, coats, and mittens, but with the inevitable sniffles, colds, and generally cranky behavior that can occur in young children. For most children, preschool is their first time away from home and family for an extended period of time. A major portion of a preschool teacher's day is spent helping children adjust to being away from home and encouraging them to play together. This is especially true at the beginning of the school year. They may need to gently reassure children who become frightened or homesick.

In both full-day and half-day programs, preschool teachers supervise snack time, helping children learn how to eat properly and clean up after themselves. Proper hygiene is also stressed. Other activities include storytelling, music, and simple arts and crafts projects. Full-day programs involve a lunch period and at least one nap period. Programs usually have high-energy activities interspersed with calmer ones. Even though the children take naps, preschool teachers must be energetic throughout the day, ready to face with good cheer the many challenges and demands of young children.

Preschool teachers also work with each child's parents. It is not unusual for parents to come to preschool and observe a child or go on a field trip with the class, and preschool teachers often take these opportunities to discuss the progress of each child as well as any specific problems or concerns. Scheduled meetings are available for parents who cannot visit the school during the day. Solutions to fairly serious problems are worked out in tandem with the parents, often with the aid of the director of the preschool, or in the case of an elementary school kindergarten, with the principal or headmaster.

Kindergarten teachers usually have their own classrooms, made up exclusively of five-year-olds. Although these teachers don't have to plan activities for a wide range of ages, they need to consider individual developmental interests, abilities, and backgrounds represented by the students. Kindergarten teachers usually spend more time helping students with academic skills than do other preschool teachers. While a teacher of a two-, three-, and four-year-old classroom may focus more on socializing and building confidence in students through play and activities, kindergarten teachers often develop activities that help five-year-olds acquire the skills they will need in grade school, such as introductory activities on numbers, reading, and writing.

REQUIREMENTS

High School

To prepare for this type of career, you should take developmental psychology, home economics, and classes that involve child care, such as family and consumer science. You'll also need a fundamental understanding of the general subjects you'll be introducing to preschool students, so take English, science, and math. Also, take classes in art, music, and theater to develop creative skills.

Postsecondary Training

Specific education requirements for preschool and kindergarten teachers vary from state to state and also depend on the specific guidelines of the school or district. Many schools and child care centers require preschool teachers to have a bachelor's degree in education or a related field, but others accept adults with a high school diploma and some childcare experience. Some preschool facilities offer on-the-job training to their teachers, hiring them as assistants or aides until they are sufficiently trained to work in a classroom alone. A college degree program should include coursework in a variety of liberal arts subjects, including English, history, and science as well as nutrition, child development, psychology of the young child, and sociology.

Several groups offer on-the-job training programs for prospective preschool teachers. For example, the American Montessori Society offers a career program for aspiring preschool teachers. This program requires a three-month classroom training period followed by one year of supervised on-the-job training.

Certification or Licensing

In some states, licensure may be required. Many states accept the child development associate credential (awarded by the Council for Professional Recogniton) or an associate or bachelor's degree as sufficient requirements for work in a preschool facility. Individual state boards of education can provide specific licensure information. Kindergarten teachers working in public elementary schools almost always need teaching certification similar to that required by other elementary school teachers in the school. Other types of licensure or certification may be required, depending upon the school or district. These may include first-aid or cardiopulmonary resuscitation (CPR) training.

Other Requirements

Because young children look up to adults and learn through example, it is especially important that you serve as a good role model in this profession. "Remember how important your job is," June Gannon says. "Everything you say and do will affect these children." Gannon

A kindergarten teacher leads a classroom activity. *(Jim West Photography)*

also emphasizes being respectful of the children and keeping a sense of humor. "I have patience and lots of heart for children," Gannon says. "You definitely need both."

EXPLORING

Preschools, daycare centers, and other childcare programs often hire high school students for part-time positions as aides. You may also find many volunteer opportunities to work with children. Check with your library or local literacy program about tutoring children and reading to preschoolers. Summer day camps or religious schools with preschool classes also hire high school students as counselors or counselors-in-training. Discussing the field with preschool teachers and observing in their classes are other good ways to discover specific job information and explore your aptitude for this career.

EMPLOYERS

There are approximately 430,000 preschool teachers employed in the United States, as well as 170,000 kindergarten teachers. Six of every 10 mothers of children under the age of six are in the labor force, and the number is rising. Both government and the private sector are working to fill the enormous need for quality childcare. Preschool teachers will find many job opportunities in private and public preschools, including daycare centers, government-funded learning programs, churches, and Montessori schools. They may find work in a small center, or with a large preschool with many students and classrooms. Preschool franchises, like Primrose Schools and Kids 'R' Kids International, are also providing more opportunities for preschool teachers.

STARTING OUT

Before becoming a preschool teacher, June Gannon gained a lot of experience in child care. "I have worked as a special education aide and have taken numerous classes in childhood education," she says. "I am a sign language interpreter and have taught deaf children in a public school inclusion program."

If you hope to become a preschool teacher, you can contact child care centers, nursery schools, Head Start programs, and other preschool facilities to identify job opportunities. Often jobs for preschool teachers are listed in the classified section of newspapers. In addition, many school districts and state boards of education maintain job listings of available teaching positions. If no permanent positions are available at preschools, you may be able to find opportunities to work as a substitute teacher. Most preschools and kindergartens maintain a substitute list and refer to it frequently.

ADVANCEMENT

Many teachers advance by becoming more skillful in what they do. Skilled preschool teachers, especially those with additional training, usually receive salary increases as they become more experienced. A few preschool teachers with administrative ability and an interest in administrative work advance to the position of director. Administrators need to have at least a master's degree in child development or a related field and have to meet any state or federal licensing regulations. Some become directors of Head Start programs or other government programs. A relatively small number of experienced preschool teachers open their own facilities. This entails not only the ability to be an effective administrator but also the knowledge of how to operate a business. Kindergarten teachers sometimes have the opportunity to earn more money by teaching at a higher grade level in the elementary school. This salary increase is especially the case when a teacher moves from a half-day kindergarten program to a full-day grade school classroom.

EARNINGS

Although there have been some attempts to correct the discrepancies in salaries between preschool teachers and other teachers, salaries in this profession tend to be lower than teaching positions in public elementary and high schools. Because some preschool programs are only in the morning or afternoon, many preschool teachers work only part time. As part-time workers, they often do not receive medical insurance or other benefits and may get paid minimum wage to start.

According to the U.S. Department of Labor, preschool teachers earned a median salary of $22,680 a year in 2006. Annual salaries for these workers ranged from less than $14,870 to $39,960 or more. The department reports that kindergarten teachers (which the department classifies separately from preschool teachers) earned median annual salaries of $43,580 in 2006. The lowest 10 percent earned less than $28,590, while the highest 10 percent earned $71,410 or more.

WORK ENVIRONMENT

Preschool teachers spend much of their work day on their feet in a classroom or on a playground. Facilities vary from a single room to large buildings. Class sizes also vary; some preschools serve only a handful of children, while others serve several hundred. Classrooms may be crowded and noisy, but anyone who loves children will enjoy all the activity. "The best part about working with children," June Gannon says, "is the laughter, the fun, the enjoyment of watching the children grow physically, emotionally, and intellectually."

Many children do not go to preschool all day, so work may be part time. Part-time employees generally work between 18 and 30 hours a week, while full-time employees work 35–40 hours a week. Part-time work gives the employee flexibility, and for many, this is one of the advantages of the job. Some preschool teachers teach both morning and afternoon classes, going through the same schedule and lesson plans with two sets of students.

OUTLOOK

Employment opportunities for preschool teachers are expected to increase about as fast as the average for all occupations through 2016, according to the U.S. Department of Labor. Specific job opportunities vary from state to state and depend on demographic characteristics and level of government funding. Jobs should be available at private child-care centers, nursery schools, Head Start facilities, public and private kindergartens, and laboratory schools connected with universities and colleges. In the past, the majority of preschool teachers were female, and although this continues to be the case, more males are becoming involved in early childhood education.

One-third of all child-care workers leave their centers each year, often because of the low pay and lack of benefits. This will mean plenty of job openings for preschool teachers and possibly improved benefit plans, as centers attempt to retain qualified preschool teachers.

Employment for all teachers, including preschool teachers, will vary by region and state. The U.S. Department of Labor predicts that southern and western states, particularly Nevada, Arizona, Texas, and Georgia, will have strong increases in enrollments, while schools located in the northeast will have declining enrollment.

FOR MORE INFORMATION

For information on training programs, contact
American Montessori Society
281 Park Avenue South, 6th Floor
New York, NY 10010-6102
Tel: 212-358-1250
http://www.amshq.org

For information about certification, contact
Council for Professional Recognition
2460 16th Street, NW
Washington, DC 20009-3575

Tel: 800-424-4310
http://www.cdacouncil.org

For general information on preschool teaching careers, contact
National Association for the Education of Young Children
1509 16th Street, NW
Washington, DC 20036-1426
Tel: 800-424-2460
http://www.naeyc.org

*For information about student memberships and training oppor-
tunities, contact*
National Association of Child Care Professionals
PO Box 90723
Austin, TX 78709-0723
Tel: 800-537-1118
Email: admin@naccp.org
http://www.naccp.org

School Administrators

OVERVIEW

School administrators are leaders who plan and set goals related to the educational, administrative, and counseling programs of schools. They coordinate and evaluate the activities of teachers and other school personnel to ensure that they adhere to deadlines and budget requirements and meet established objectives. There are approximately 332,000 school administrators employed in the United States.

HISTORY

The history of school administration is almost as old as the history of education itself. The first American colonists of the 17th century set up schools in their homes. In the 18th century, groups of prosperous parents established separate schools and employed schoolmasters. In these small early schools, the teachers were also the administrators, charged with the operation of the school as well as with the instruction of the pupils.

In the early 1800s, the importance of education gained recognition among people from all classes of society and the government became involved in providing schooling without cost to all children. Schools grew larger, a more complex system of education evolved, and there developed a demand for educators specializing in the area of administration.

In the United States, each state has its own school system, headed by a state superintendent or commissioner of education who works in conjunction with the state board of education. The states are divided into local school districts, which may vary in size from a large urban area to a sparsely populated area containing a single classroom of children. The board of education in each district elects a professionally trained superintendent or supervising principal to administer the local schools. In most school districts the superintendent has one or more assistants, and in a very large district the superintendent may also be assisted by business managers, directors of curriculum, or research and testing personnel. Individual schools within a district are usually headed by a school principal and one or more assistant principals. The administrative staff of a very large secondary school may also include deans, registrars, department heads, counselors, and others.

The problems of school administrators today are much more complex than in the past and require political as well as administrative skills. School leaders are confronted by such volatile issues as desegregation, school closings and reduced enrollments, contract negotiations with teachers, student and staff safety, and greatly increased costs coupled with public resistance to higher taxes.

THE JOB

The occupation of school administrator includes school district superintendents, assistant superintendents, school principals, and assistant principals. Private schools also have administrators, often known as *school directors* or *headmasters*. Administrators in either public or private schools are responsible for the smooth, efficient operation of an individual school or an entire school system, depending on the size and type of the school or the size of the district. They make plans, set goals, and supervise and coordinate the activities of teachers and other school personnel in carrying out those plans within the established time framework and budget allowance. The general job descriptions that follow refer to administrators in the public school system.

School principals far outnumber the other school administrators, are the most familiar to the students, and are often seen as disciplinarians. Principals spend a great deal of time resolving conflicts that students and teachers may have with one another, with parents, or with school board policies, but their authority extends to many other matters. They are responsible for the performance of an individual school, directing and coordinating educational, administrative, and counseling activities according to standards set by the superintendent and the board of education. They hire and assign teachers and other staff, help them improve their skills, and evaluate their performance. They plan and evaluate the instructional programs jointly with teachers. Periodically, they visit classrooms to observe the effectiveness of the teachers and teaching methods, review educational objectives, and examine learning materials, always seeking ways to improve the quality of instruction.

Principals are responsible for the registration, schedules, and attendance of pupils. In cases of severe educational or behavioral problems, they may confer with teachers, students, parents, and counselors and recommend corrective measures. They cooperate with community organizations, colleges, and other schools to coordinate educational services. They oversee the day-to-day operations of the school building and requisition and allocate equipment, supplies, and instructional materials.

A school principal's duties necessitate a great deal of paperwork: filling out forms, preparing administrative reports, and keeping records. They also spend much of each day meeting with people: teachers and other school personnel, colleagues, students, parents, and other members of the community.

In larger schools, most often secondary schools, principals may have one or more assistants. *Assistant principals,* who may be known as *deans of students,* provide counseling for individuals or student groups related to personal problems, educational or vocational objectives, and social and recreational activities. They often handle discipline, interviewing students, and taking whatever action is necessary in matters such as truancy and delinquency. Assistant principals generally plan and supervise social and recreational programs and coordinate other school activities.

Superintendents manage the affairs of an entire school district, which may range in size from a small town with a handful of schools to a city with a population of millions. Superintendents must be elected by the board of education to oversee and coordinate the activities of all the schools in the district in accordance with board of education standards. They select and employ staff and negotiate contracts. They develop and administer budgets, the acquisition and maintenance of school buildings, and the purchase and distribution of school supplies and equipment. They coordinate related activities with other school districts and agencies. They speak before community and civic groups and try to enlist their support. In addition, they collect statistics, prepare reports, enforce compulsory attendance, and oversee the operation of the school transportation system and provision of health services.

School district superintendents usually have one or more assistants or deputies, whose duties vary depending on the size and nature of the school system. *Assistant superintendents* may have charge of a particular geographic area or may specialize in activities pertaining, for example, to budget, personnel, or curriculum development.

Boards of education vary in their level of authority and their method of appointment or election to the post of board member. Normally, board members are elected from leaders in the community in business and education. It is not uncommon to have the board selected by the mayor or other city administrator.

REQUIREMENTS
High School
School administration calls for a high level of education and experience. For this reason, you should begin preparing for the job by taking a wide range of college preparatory courses, including English, mathematics, science, music, art, and history. Computer science and business classes will also be beneficial. A broad secondary school education will help you as you pursue your college degrees and gain admittance into strong colleges of education.

Postsecondary Training
Principals and assistant principals are generally required to have a master's degree in educational administration in addition to several years' experience as a classroom teacher.

School superintendents usually must have had graduate training in educational administration, preferably at the doctoral level. Some larger districts require a law degree or a business degree in addition to a graduate degree in education. Candidates for the position of school superintendent generally must have accumulated previous experience as an administrator.

The National Council for Accreditation of Teacher Education and the Educational Leadership Constituent Council accredit graduate programs in educational administration. Programs are designed specifically for elementary school principals, secondary school principals, or school district superintendents and include such courses as school management, school law, curriculum development and evaluation, and personnel administration. A semester of internship and field experience are extremely valuable.

Certification or Licensing
Licensure of school administrators is mandatory in all 50 states and the District of Columbia. Requirements to become licensed may include U.S. citizenship or state residency, graduate training in educational administration, experience, and good health and character. In some states, candidates must pass a qualifying examination. You can obtain information on specific requirements from the department of education in your state.

The Interstate School Leaders Licensure Consortium (ISLLC) developed and established standards, assessments, professional development, and licensing procedures for school leaders. The ISLLC aimed to raise the bar for school leaders to enter and remain in the profession and to reshape concepts of educational leadership. While the ISLLC is no longer in operation, its intentions remain strong—35 states have either adopted or adapted the ISLLC standards and are in different stages of implementing them.

The Educational Testing Service (ETS) offers the School Leaders Licensure Assessment test, which measures whether or not entry-level principals and other school leaders are fit for professional practice. The ETS also offers the School Superintendent Assessment test, which measures an administrator's understanding of ISLLC standards.

Other Requirements

You should have leadership skills necessary for keeping the school operating smoothly. You also need good communication skills and the ability to get along with many different types and ages of people. Strong self-motivation and self-confidence are important for putting your plans into action, and for withstanding criticism.

EXPLORING

If you've been attending a private or public school, you're already very familiar with the nature of education and already know many great resources of information, such as your own teachers and school administrators. Talk to your teachers about their work, and offer to assist them with some projects before or after school. School counselors can offer vocational guidance, provide occupational materials, and help students plan appropriate programs of study.

You can gain experience in the education field by getting a summer job as a camp counselor or day care center aide, working with a scouting group, volunteering to coach a youth athletic team, tutoring younger students, or helping with religious instruction classes at your church, synagogue, or mosque.

EMPLOYERS

There are approximately 332,000 education administrators employed throughout the United States. Principals work in either public or private schools at the elementary or secondary level. Superintendents work for a school district, which may include many elementary and secondary schools. School administrators are also needed for large preschools and job training programs. See the article "College Administrators" to learn about opportunities with colleges and universities.

STARTING OUT

Most school administrators enter the field as teachers. College and university career services offices may help place you in your first teaching job, or you may apply directly to a local school system. Teachers, of course, must meet the requirements for state licensure. Many school districts and state departments of education maintain job listings that notify potential teachers and administrators of openings. Qualified candidates may also come from other administrative jobs, such as curriculum specialist, financial adviser, or director of audiovisual aids, libraries, arts, or special education. The most important qualification is having experience in organizing and supervising school programs and activities.

ADVANCEMENT

A teacher may be promoted directly to principal, but more often teachers begin as assistant principals and in time are promoted. Experienced administrators may advance to assistant superintendent and then superintendent. In fact, many school superintendents are former principals who worked their way up the administrative ladder. Each increase in responsibility usually carries a corresponding salary increase.

EARNINGS

The income of school administrators depends on the position, the level of responsibility, and the size and geographic location of the school or school district.

According to the U.S. Department of Labor, the median salary for education administrators was $77,740 in 2006. The lowest paid 10 percent of administrators earned $51,320 or less per year, while the highest paid made $112,990 or more annually.

School administrators also receive benefits including health insurance, retirement plans, and vacation and sick leave.

WORK ENVIRONMENT

Most school administrators work a standard 40-hour week, although they often attend meetings or handle urgent matters in the evenings or on weekends. The job requires year-round attention. One-third of school administrators work more than 40 hours a week.

Administrators work in pleasant office environments, usually at a desk. At times, however, they attend meetings elsewhere with PTA members, the school board, and civic groups. Principals and their assistants periodically sit in on classes, attend school assemblies and events, and conduct inspections of the school's physical facilities.

OUTLOOK

Employment for school administrators is expected to grow about as fast as the average for all occupations through 2016, according to the U.S. Department of Labor. Elementary and secondary school enrollments are expected to grow more slowly over the next decade, and many potential administrators are steering clear of the field due to increasing job responsibilities and high stress (60 percent of school superintendents reported being "very stressed" in their jobs, according to a recent study by the American Association of School Administrators). Employment opportunities should be best in the South and West—areas in which the population is growing the fastest.

The number of school administrators employed is determined to a large extent by state and local expenditures for education. Budget cuts affect the number of available positions in administration, and how an administrator can perform his or her job. Administrators in the coming years will have to be creative in finding funds. They are also faced with developing additional programs for children as more parents work outside the home. Schools may be expected to help care for children before and after regular school hours.

Administrators may also oversee smaller learning environments in the coming years. Research has proven that smaller classrooms and more individual attention not only improve education but help educators identify students with personal and emotional problems. To keep students safe from violence, drug abuse, and street gangs, administrators may develop more individualized education.

FOR MORE INFORMATION

For articles and news reports about the career of school administrator, contact the following organizations:

American Association of School Administrators
801 North Quincy Street
Arlington, VA 22203-1730
Tel: 703-528-0700

Email: info@aasa.org
http://www.aasa.org

For information on assessment tests for school administrators, contact
Educational Testing Service
Rosedale Road
Princeton, NJ 08541
Tel: 609-921-9000
http://www.ets.org

National Association of Elementary School Principals
1615 Duke Street
Alexandria, VA 22314-3406
Tel: 800-386-2377
Email: naesp@naesp.org
http://www.naesp.org

National Association of Secondary School Principals
1904 Association Drive
Reston, VA 20191-1537
Tel: 703-860-0200
Email: membership@principals.org
http://www.nassp.org

Secondary School Teachers

OVERVIEW

Secondary school teachers teach students in grades seven–12. Specializing in one subject area, such as English or math, these teachers work with five or more groups of students during the day. They lecture, direct discussions, and test students' knowledge with exams, essays, and homework assignments. There are close to 1.1 million secondary school teachers employed in the United States.

HISTORY

Early secondary education was typically based upon training students to enter the clergy. Benjamin Franklin pioneered the idea of a broader secondary education with the creation of the academy, which offered a flexible curriculum and a wide variety of academic subjects.

It was not until the 19th century, however, that children of different social classes commonly attended school into the secondary grades. The first English Classical School, which was to become the model for public high schools throughout the country, was established in 1821 in Boston. An adjunct to the high school, the junior high school was conceived by Dr. Charles W. Eliot, president of Harvard. In a speech before the National Education Association in 1888, he recommended that secondary studies be started two years earlier than was the custom. The first such school opened in 1908, in Columbus, Ohio. Another opened a year later in Berkeley, California. By the early 20th century, secondary school attendance was made mandatory in the United States.

THE JOB

Many successful people credit secondary school teachers with helping guide them into college, careers, and other endeavors. The teachers' primary responsibility is to educate students in a specific subject. But secondary teachers also inform students about colleges, occupations, and such varied subjects as the arts, health, and relationships.

Secondary school teachers may teach in a traditional area, such as science, English, history, and math, or they may teach more specialized classes, such as information technology, business, and theater. Many secondary schools are expanding their course offerings to serve the individual interests of their students more effectively. "School-to-work" programs, which are vocational education programs designed for high school students and recent graduates, involve lab work and demonstrations to prepare students for highly technical jobs. Though secondary teachers are likely to be assigned to one specific grade level, they may be required to teach students in other grades. For example, a secondary school mathematics teacher may teach algebra to a class of ninth-graders one period and trigonometry to high school seniors the next.

In the classroom, secondary school teachers rely on a variety of teaching methods. They spend a great deal of time lecturing, but they also facilitate student discussion and develop projects and activities to interest the students in the subject. They show films and videos, use computers and the Internet, and bring in guest speakers. They assign essays, presentations, and other projects. Each individual subject calls upon particular approaches, and may involve laboratory experiments, role-playing exercises, shop work, and field trips.

Outside of the classroom, secondary school teachers prepare lectures, lesson plans, and exams. They evaluate student work and calculate grades. In the process of planning their class, secondary school teachers read textbooks, novels, and workbooks to determine reading assignments; photocopy notes, articles, and other handouts; and develop grading policies. They also continue to study alternative and traditional teaching methods to hone their skills. They prepare students for special events and conferences and submit student work to competitions. Many secondary school teachers also serve as sponsors to student organizations in their field. For example, a French teacher may sponsor the French club and a journalism teacher may advise the yearbook staff. Some secondary school teachers also have the opportunity for extracurricular work as athletic coaches or drama coaches. Teachers also monitor students during lunch or break times and sit in on study halls. They may also accompany student groups on field trips, competitions, and events. Some teachers also have the opportunity to escort students on educational vacations to foreign countries, to Washington, D.C. and to other major U.S. cities. Secondary school teachers attend faculty meetings, meetings with parents, and state and national teacher conferences.

Some teachers explore their subject area outside of the requirements of the job. *English* and *writing teachers* may publish in magazines and journals, *business* and *technology teachers* may have small businesses of their own, *music teachers* may perform and record their music, *art teachers* may show work in galleries, and *sign-language teachers* may do freelance interpreting.

REQUIREMENTS

High School

You should follow your guidance counselor's college preparatory program and take advanced classes in such subjects as English, science, math, and government. You should also explore an extracurricular activity, such as theater, sports, and debate, so that you can offer these additional skills to future employers. If you're already aware of which subject you'd like to teach, take all the available courses in that area. You should also take speech and composition courses to develop your communication skills.

Postsecondary Training

There are more than 500 accredited teacher education programs in the United States. Most of these programs are designed to meet the certification requirements for the state in which they're located. Some states may require that you pass a test before being admitted to an education program. You may choose to major in your subject area while taking required education courses, or you may major in secondary education with a concentration in your subject area. You'll probably have advisers (both in education and in your chosen specialty) to help you select courses.

In addition to a degree, a training period of student teaching in an actual classroom environment is usually required. Students are placed in schools to work with full-time teachers. During this period, undergraduate students observe the ways in which lessons are presented and the classroom is managed, learn how to keep records of such details as attendance and grades, and get actual experience in handling the class, both under supervision and alone.

Besides licensure and courses in education, prospective high school teachers usually need 24–36 credit hours of college work in the subject they wish to teach. Some states require a master's

The Most Popular Bachelor's Degrees, 2004–05

1. Business (311,574 degrees conferred)
2. Social Sciences and History (156,892)
3. Education (105,451)
4. Psychology (85,614)
5. Visual and Performing Arts (80,955)
6. Health Professions and Related Clinical Sciences (80,685)
7. Communications, Journalism, and Related Programs (72,715)
8. Engineering (64,906)
9. Biological and Biomedical Sciences (64,611)
10. English Language and Literature/Letters (54,379)
11. Computer and Information Sciences (54,111)
12. Liberal Arts and Sciences, General Studies, and Humanities (43,751)
13. Security and Protective Services (30,723)
14. Multi/Interdisciplinary Studies (30,243)
15. Agriculture and Natural Resources (23,002)

Source: National Center for Education Statistics

degree; teachers with master's degrees can earn higher salaries. Private schools generally do not require an education degree.

Certification or Licensing
Public school teachers must be licensed under regulations established by the department of education of the state in which they teach. Not all states require licensure for teachers in private or parochial schools. When you've received your teaching degree, you may request that a transcript of your college record be sent to the licensure section of the state department of education. If you have met licensure requirements, you will receive a certificate and thus be eligible to teach in the public schools of the state. In some states, you may have to take additional tests. If you move to another state, you will have to resubmit college transcripts, as well as comply with any other regulations in the new state to be able to teach there.

Other Requirements
Working as a secondary school teacher, you'll need to have respect for young people and a genuine interest in their success in life. You'll

also need patience; adolescence can be a troubling time for children, and these troubles often affect behavior and classroom performance. Because you'll be working with students who are at very impressionable ages, you should serve as a good role model. You should also be well organized, as you'll have to keep track of the work and progress of many students.

EXPLORING

By going to high school, you've already gained a good sense of the daily work of a secondary school teacher. But the requirements of a teacher extend far beyond the classroom, so ask to spend some time with one of your teachers after school, and ask to look at lecture notes and record-keeping procedures. Interview your teachers about the amount of work that goes into preparing a class and directing an extracurricular activity. To get some firsthand teaching experience, volunteer for a peer tutoring program. Many other teaching opportunities may exist in your community. Look into coaching an athletic team at the YMCA, counseling at a summer camp, teaching an art course at a community center, or assisting with a community theater production.

EMPLOYERS

Approximately 1.1 million secondary school teachers are employed in the United States. Secondary school teachers are needed at public and private schools, including parochial schools, juvenile detention centers, vocational schools, and schools of the arts. They work in middle schools, junior high schools, and high schools. Though some rural areas maintain schools, most secondary schools are in towns and cities of all sizes. Teachers are also finding opportunities in charter schools, which are smaller, deregulated schools that receive public funding.

STARTING OUT

After completing the teacher certification process, including your months of student teaching, you'll work with your college's career services office to find a full-time position. The departments of education of some states maintain listings of job openings. Many schools advertise teaching positions in the classifieds of the state's major newspapers. You may also directly contact the principals and superintendents of the schools in which you'd like to work. While waiting for full-time work, you can work as a substitute teacher. In urban areas with many schools, you may be able to substitute full time.

ADVANCEMENT

Most teachers advance simply by becoming more of an expert in the job that they have chosen. There is usually an increase in salary as teachers acquire experience. Additional training or study can also bring an increase in salary.

A few teachers with management ability and interest in administrative work may advance to the position of principal. Others may advance into supervisory positions, and some may become *helping teachers* who are charged with the responsibility of helping other teachers find appropriate instructional materials and develop certain phases of their courses of study. Others may go into teacher education at a college or university. For most of these positions, additional education is required. Some teachers also make lateral moves into other education-related positions such as guidance counselor or resource room teacher.

EARNINGS

Most teachers are contracted to work nine months out of the year, though some contracts are made for 10 or a full 12 months. (When regular school is not in session, teachers are expected to conduct summer teaching, planning, or other school-related work.) In most cases, teachers have the option of prorating their salary up to 52 weeks.

According to the U.S. Department of Labor, the median annual salary for secondary school teachers was $47,740 in 2006. The lowest 10 percent earned less than $31,760; the highest 10 percent earned $76,100 or more. According to the American Federation of Teachers, beginning teachers earned an average salary of $31,753 a year in 2004–05. Teachers can also supplement their earnings through teaching summer classes, coaching sports, sponsoring a club, or other extracurricular work.

On behalf of the teachers, unions bargain with schools over contract conditions such as wages, hours, and benefits. A majority of teachers join the American Federation of Teachers or the National Education Association. Depending on the state, teachers usually receive a retirement plan, sick leave, and health and life insurance. Some systems grant teachers sabbatical leave.

WORK ENVIRONMENT

Although the job of the secondary school teacher is not overly strenuous, it can be tiring and trying. Secondary school teachers must stand for many hours each day, do a lot of talking, show energy and enthusiasm, and handle discipline problems. But they also have the reward of guiding their students as they make decisions about their lives and futures.

Secondary school teachers work under generally pleasant conditions, though some older schools may have poor heating and electrical systems. Though violence in schools has decreased in recent years, media coverage of the violence has increased, along with student fears. In most schools, students are prepared to learn and to perform the work that's required of them. But in some schools, students may be dealing with gangs, drugs, poverty, and other problems, so the environment can be tense and emotional.

School hours are generally 8 A.M. to 3 P.M., but teachers work more than 40 hours a week teaching, preparing for classes, grading papers, and directing extracurricular activities. As a coach, or as a music or drama director, teachers may have to work some evenings and weekends. Many teachers enroll in master's or doctoral programs and take evening and summer courses to continue their education.

OUTLOOK

The U.S. Department of Education predicts that employment for secondary teachers will grow more slowly than the average for all occupations through 2016 due to predicted enrollment declines during the next decade. Additionally, many prospective teachers are steering clear of this career due to the low salaries that are paid to secondary school teachers. Higher salaries will be necessary to attract new teachers and retain experienced ones, along with other changes such as smaller classroom sizes and safer schools. Other challenges for the profession involve attracting more men into teaching. The percentage of male teachers at this level continues to decline.

In order to improve education for all children, changes are being considered by some districts. Some private companies are managing public schools. Though it is believed that a private company can afford to provide better facilities, faculty, and equipment, this hasn't been proven. Teacher organizations are concerned about taking school management away from communities and turning it over to remote corporate headquarters. Charter schools and voucher programs are two other controversial alternatives to traditional public education. Charter schools, which are small schools that are publicly funded but not guided by the rules and regulations of traditional public schools, are viewed by some as places of innovation and improved educational methods; others see charter schools as ill-equipped and unfairly funded with money that could better benefit local school districts. Vouchers, which exist only in a few cities, allow students to attend private schools courtesy of tuition vouchers; these vouchers are paid for with public tax dollars. In theory, the vouchers allow for more choices in education for poor and minority students, but private schools still have the option of being highly selective in their admissions. Teacher organizations, however, see some danger in giving public funds to unregulated private schools.

FOR MORE INFORMATION

For information about careers and current issues affecting teachers, contact or visit the Web sites of the following organizations:
American Federation of Teachers
555 New Jersey Avenue, NW
Washington, DC 20001-2029
Tel: 202-879-4400
Email: online@aft.org
http://www.aft.org

National Education Association
1201 16th Street, NW
Washington, DC 20036-3290
Tel: 202-833-4000
http://www.nea.org

For information on accredited teacher education programs, contact
National Council for Accreditation of Teacher Education
2010 Massachusetts Avenue, NW, Suite 500
Washington, DC 20036-1023
Tel: 202-466-7496
Email: ncate@ncate.org
http://www.ncate.org

This Web site serves as a clearinghouse for men interested in becoming teachers.
MenTeach
http://www.menteach.org

Special Education Teachers

OVERVIEW

Special education teachers teach students aged three through 21 who have a variety of disabilities. These teachers design individualized education plans and work with students one-on-one to help them learn academic subjects and life skills. Approximately 459,000 special education teachers are employed in the United States.

HISTORY

Modern special education traces its origins to 16th-century Spain, where Pedro Ponce de Leon and Juan Pablo Bonet taught deaf students to read and write. In the late 18th century in Paris, Valentin Huay established the first institute for blind children. The first U.S. schools for the blind were founded in 1832 in Boston and New York.

By the early 19th century, attempts were made to educate the mentally handicapped. Edouard Sequin, a French psychiatrist, established the first school for the mentally handicapped in 1939 in Orange, N.J.

In the first half of the 20th century, special education became increasingly popular in the United States. By the 1960s and early 1970s, parents began to lobby state and local officials for improved special education programs for their children with disabilities. To address continuing inequities in the public education of special needs students, Congress passed the Education for All Handicapped Children Act (Public Law 94-142) in 1975. The Act required public schools to provide disabled students with a "free appropriate education" in the "least restrictive environment" possible. The Act was reauthorized in 1990, 1997, and 2004 and renamed the Individuals with Disabilities Education Act. This Act allows approximately 6.5 million children (roughly 10 percent of all school-aged children) to receive special education services from highly trained special education teachers.

THE JOB

Special education teachers instruct students who have a variety of disabilities. Their students may have physical disabilities, such as vision, hearing, or orthopedic impairment. They may also have learning disabilities or serious emotional disturbances. Although it is less common, special education teachers sometimes work with students who are gifted and talented, children who have limited proficiency in English, children who have communicable diseases, or children who are neglected and abused.

In order to teach special education students, these teachers design and modify instruction so that it is tailored to individual student needs. Teachers collaborate with school psychologists, social workers, parents, and occupational, physical, and speech-language therapists to develop a specially designed program called an Individualized Education Program (IEP) for each of their students. The IEP sets personalized goals for a student, based upon his or her learning style and ability, and outlines specific steps to prepare him or her for employment or postsecondary schooling.

Special education teachers teach at a pace that is dictated by the individual needs and abilities of their students. Unlike most regular classes, special education classes do not have an established curriculum that is taught to all students at the same time. Because students' abilities vary widely, instruction is individualized and it is part of the teacher's responsibility to match specific techniques with a student's learning style and abilities. They may spend much time working with students one-on-one or in small groups.

Working with different types of students requires a variety of teaching methods. Some students may need to use special equipment or skills in the classroom in order to overcome their disabilities. For example, a teacher working with a student with a physical disability might use a computer that is operated by touching a screen or by voice commands. To work with hearing-impaired students, the teacher may need to use sign language. With visually impaired students, he or she may use teaching materials that have Braille characters or large, easy-to-see type. Gifted and talented students may need additional challenging assignments, a faster learning pace, or special attention in one curriculum area, such as art or music.

In addition to teaching academic subjects, special education teachers help students develop both emotionally and socially. They work to make students as independent as possible by teaching them functional skills for daily living. They may help young children learn basic grooming, hygiene, and table manners. Older students might be taught how to balance a checkbook, follow a recipe, or use the public transportation system.

Special education teachers meet regularly with their students' parents to inform them of their child's progress and offer suggestions of how to promote learning at home. They may also meet with school administrators, social workers, psychologists, various types of therapists, and students' general education teachers.

The current trend in education is to integrate students with disabilities into regular classrooms to the extent that it is possible and beneficial to them. This is often called "mainstreaming." As mainstreaming becomes increasingly common, special education teachers frequently work with general education teachers in general education classrooms. They may help adapt curriculum materials and teaching techniques to meet the needs of students with disabilities and offer guidance on dealing with students' emotional and behavioral problems.

In addition to working with students, special education teachers are responsible for a certain amount of paperwork. They document each student's progress and may fill out any forms that are required by the school system or the government.

REQUIREMENTS

High School
If you are considering a career as a special education teacher, you should focus on courses that will prepare you for college. These classes include natural and social sciences, mathematics, and English. Speech classes would also be a good choice for improving your communication skills. Finally, classes in psychology might be helpful both to help you understand the students you will eventually teach, and prepare you for college-level psychology course work.

Postsecondary Training
All states require that teachers have at least a bachelor's degree and that they complete a prescribed number of subject and education credits. It is increasingly common for special education teachers to complete an additional fifth year of training after they receive their

bachelor's degree. Many states require special education teachers to get a master's degree in special education.

There are approximately 800 colleges and universities in the United States that offer programs in special education, including undergraduate, master's, and doctoral programs. These programs include general and specialized courses in special education, including educational psychology, legal issues of special education, child growth and development, and knowledge and skills needed for teaching students with disabilities. The student typically spends the last year of the program student-teaching in an actual classroom, under the supervision of a licensed teacher.

Certification or Licensing
All states require that special education teachers be licensed, although the particulars of licensing vary by state. In some states, these teachers must first be certified as elementary or secondary school teachers, then meet specific requirements to teach special education. Some states offer general special education licensure; others license several different subspecialties within special education. Some states allow special education teachers to transfer their license from one state to another, but many still require these teachers to pass licensing requirements for that state.

Other Requirements
To be successful in this field, you need to have many of the same personal characteristics as regular classroom teachers: the ability to communicate, a broad knowledge of the arts, sciences, and history, and a love of children. In addition, you will need a great deal of patience and persistence. You need to be creative, flexible, cooperative, and accepting of differences in others. Finally, you need to be emotionally stable and consistent in your dealings with students.

EXPLORING

There are a number of ways to explore the field of special education. One of the first and easiest is to approach a special education teacher at his or her school and ask to talk about the job. Perhaps the teacher could provide a tour of the special education classroom, or allow you to visit while a class is in session.

You might also want to become acquainted with special-needs students at your own school or become involved in a school or community mentoring program for these students. There may also be other opportunities for volunteer work or part-time jobs in schools, community agencies, camps, or residential facilities that will allow you to work with persons with disabilities.

EMPLOYERS

There are approximately 459,000 special education teachers employed in the United States. The majority of special education teachers teach in public and private schools. Others work in state education agencies, homebound or hospital environments, or residential facilities.

STARTING OUT

Because public school systems are by far the largest employers of special education teachers, this is where you should begin your job search.

You can also use your college's career services center to locate job leads. This may prove a very effective place to begin. You may also write to your state's department of education for information on placement and regulations, or contact state employment offices to inquire about job openings. Applying directly to local school systems can sometimes be effective. Even if a school system does not have an immediate opening, it will usually keep your resume on file should a vacancy occur.

ADVANCEMENT

Advancement opportunities for special education teachers, as for regular classroom teachers, are fairly limited. They may take the form of higher wages, better facilities, or more prestige. In some cases, these teachers advance to become supervisors or administrators, although this may require continued education on the teacher's part. Another option is for special education teachers to earn advanced degrees and become instructors at the college level.

EARNINGS

In some school districts, salaries for special education teachers follow the same scale as general education teachers. According to the U.S. Department of Labor, salaries for special education teachers ranged from less than $31,320 to more than $80,170 in 2006. Preschool, kindergarten, and elementary schools paid an average of $46,360, middle schools, $47,650; and secondary schools, $48,330. Private school teachers usually earn less than their public school counterparts. Teachers can supplement their annual salaries by becoming an activity sponsor, or through summer work.

Other school districts pay their special education teachers on a separate scale, which is usually higher than that of general education teachers.

Regardless of the salary scale, special education teachers usually receive a complete benefits package, which includes health and life insurance, paid holidays and vacations, and a pension plan.

WORK ENVIRONMENT

Special education teachers usually work from 7:30 or 8:00 A.M. to 3:00 or 3:30 P.M. Like most teachers, however, they typically spend several hours in the evening grading papers, completing paperwork, or preparing lessons for the next day. Altogether, most special education teachers work more than the standard 40 hours per week.

Although some schools offer year-round classes for students, the majority of special education teachers work the traditional 10-month school year, with a two-month vacation in the summer. Many teachers find this work schedule very appealing, as it gives them the opportunity to pursue personal interests or additional education during the summer break. Teachers typically also get a week off at Christmas and for spring break.

Special education teachers work in a variety of settings in schools, including both ordinary and specially equipped classrooms, resource rooms, and therapy rooms. Some schools have newer and better facilities for special education than others. Although it is less common, some teachers work in residential facilities or tutor students who are homebound or hospitalized.

Working with special education students can be very demanding, due to their physical and emotional needs. Teachers may fight a constant battle to keep certain students, particularly those with behavior disorders, under control. Other students, such as those with mental impairments or learning disabilities, learn so slowly that it may seem as if they are making no progress. The special education teacher must deal daily with frustration, setbacks, and classroom disturbances.

These teachers must also contend with heavy workloads, including a great deal of paperwork to document each student's progress. In addition, they may sometimes be faced with irate parents who feel that their child is not receiving proper treatment or an adequate education.

The positive side of this job is that special education teachers help students overcome their disabilities and learn to be as functional as possible. For a special education teacher, knowing that he or she is making a difference in a child's life can be very rewarding and emotionally fulfilling.

OUTLOOK

The field of special education is expected to grow faster than the average for all occupations through 2016, according to the U.S. Department of Labor. This demand is caused partly by the growth in the number of special education students needing services. Medical advances resulting in more survivors of illness and accidents, the rise in birth defects, especially in older pregnancies, as well as general population growth, are also significant factors for strong demand. Because of the rise in the number of youths with disabilities under the age of 21, the government has given approval for more federally funded programs. Growth of jobs in this field has also been influenced positively by legislation emphasizing training and employment for individuals with disabilities and a growing public awareness and interest in those with disabilities.

Finally, there is a fairly high turnover rate in this field, as many special education teachers find the work too stressful and switch to mainstream teaching or change jobs altogether. Many job openings will arise out of a need to replace teachers who leave their positions. There is a shortage of qualified teachers in rural areas and in the inner city. Jobs will also be plentiful for teachers who specialize in speech and language impairments, multiple disabilities, severe disabilities such as autism, learning disabilities, and early childhood intervention. Bilingual teachers with multicultural experience will be in high demand.

FOR MORE INFORMATION

For information on current issues, legal cases, and conferences, contact

Council of Administrators of Special Education
Fort Valley State University
1005 State University Drive
Fort Valley, GA 31030-4313
Tel: 478-825-7667
http://www.casecec.org

For information on careers, contact
National Association of Special Education Teachers
1250 Connecticut Avenue, NW, Suite 200
Washington DC 20036-2643

Tel: 800-754-4421
Email: contactus@naset.org
http://www.naset.org

For information on special education programs sponsored by the federal government, contact
U.S. Department of Education
Office of Special Education and Rehabilitative Services
400 Maryland Avenue, SW
Washington, DC 20202-7100
Tel: 202-245-7468
http://www.ed.gov/about/offices/list/osers/index.html

For information on accredited schools, teacher certification, financial aid, and careers in special education, contact
National Clearinghouse for Professions in Special Education
http://www.special-ed-careers.org

Speech-Language Pathologists and Audiologists

OVERVIEW

Speech-language pathologists and *audiologists* help people who have speech and hearing defects. They identify the problem and use tests to further evaluate it. Speech-language pathologists try to improve the speech and language skills of clients with communications disorders. Audiologists perform tests to measure the hearing ability of clients, who may range in age from the very young to the very old. Since it is not uncommon for clients to require assistance for both speech and hearing, pathologists and audiologists may frequently work together to help clients. Some professionals decide to combine these jobs into one, working as speech-language pathologists or audiologists. Audiologists and speech-language pathologists may work for school systems, in private practice, and at clinics and other medical facilities. Other employment possibilities for these professionals include teaching at universities, and conducting research on what causes certain speech and hearing defects. There are approximately 110,000 speech-language pathologists and audiologists employed in the United States.

HISTORY

The diagnosis and treatment of speech and hearing defects is a new part of medical science. In the past, physicians were not able to help patients with these types of problems because there was usually nothing visibly wrong, and little was known about how speech and hearing were related. Until the middle of the 19th century, medical researchers did not know whether speech defects were caused by lack of hearing, or whether the patient was the victim of two separate ailments. And even if they could figure out why something was wrong, doctors still could not communicate with the patient.

QUICK FACTS

(continued)

O*NET-SOC
29-1127.00 (speech-language pathologists)
29-1121.00 (audiologists)

Alexander Graham Bell, the inventor of the telephone, provided some of the answers. His grandfather taught elocution (the art of public speaking), and Bell grew up interested in the problems of speech and hearing. It became his profession, and by 1871 Bell was lecturing to teachers of deaf people at Boston University. Soon afterward, Bell opened his own school, where he experimented with the idea of making speech visible to his pupils. If he could make them see the movements made by different human tones, they could speak by learning to produce similar vibrations. Bell's efforts not only helped deaf people of his day, but also led directly to the invention of the telephone in 1876. Probably the most famous deaf person in American history is Helen Keller, whose teacher, Anne Sullivan, applied Bell's discoveries to help Keller overcome her blindness and deafness.

THE JOB

Even though the two professions seem to blend together at times, speech-language pathology and audiology are very different from one another. However, because both speech and hearing are related to one another, a person competent in one discipline must have familiarity with the other.

The duties performed by speech-language pathologists and audiologists differ depending on education, experience, and place of employment. Most speech-language pathologists provide direct clinical services to individuals and independently develop and carry out treatment programs. In medical facilities, they may work with physicians, social workers, psychologists, and other therapists to develop and execute treatment plans. In a school environment, they develop individual or group programs, counsel parents, and sometimes help teachers with classroom activities.

Clients of speech-language pathologists include people who cannot make speech sounds, or cannot make them clearly; those with speech rhythm and fluency problems such as stuttering; people with voice quality problems, such as inappropriate pitch or harsh voice; those with problems understanding and producing language; and those with cognitive communication impairments, such as attention, memory, and problem-solving disorders. Speech-language pathologists may also work with people who have oral motor problems that cause eating and swallowing difficulties. Clients' problems may be congenital, developmental, or acquired, and caused by hearing loss, brain injury or deterioration, cerebral palsy, stroke, cleft palate, voice pathology, mental retardation, or emotional problems.

Speech-language pathologists conduct written and oral tests and use special instruments to analyze and diagnose the nature and extent of impairment. They develop an individualized plan of care, which may include automated devices and sign language. They teach clients how to make sounds, improve their voices, or increase their language skills to communicate more effectively. Speech-language pathologists help clients develop, or recover, reliable communication skills.

People who have difficulty with hearing, balance, and related problems consult audiologists, who use audiometers and other testing devices to discover the nature and extent of hearing loss. Audiologists interpret these results and may coordinate them with medical, educational, and psychological information to make a diagnosis and determine a course of treatment.

Hearing disorders can result from trauma at birth, viral infections, genetic disorders, or exposure to loud noise. Treatment may include examining and cleaning the ear canal, fitting and dispensing a hearing aid or other device, and audiologic rehabilitation (including auditory training or instruction in speech or lip reading). Audiologists provide fitting and tuning of cochlear implants and help those with implants adjust to the implant amplification systems. They also test noise levels in workplaces and conduct hearing protection programs in industrial settings, as well as in schools and communities.

Audiologists provide direct clinical services to clients and sometimes develop and implement individual treatment programs. In some environments, however, they work as members of professional teams in planning and implementing treatment plans.

In a research environment, speech pathologists and audiologists investigate communicative disorders and their causes and ways to improve clinical services. Those teaching in colleges and universities instruct students on the principles and bases of communication,

communication disorders, and clinical techniques used in speech and hearing.

Speech-language pathologists and audiologists keep records on the initial evaluation, progress, and discharge of clients to identify problems and track progress. They counsel individuals and their families on how to cope with the stress and misunderstanding that often accompany communication disorders.

REQUIREMENTS

High School

Since a college degree is a must for practicing this profession, make sure your high school classes are geared toward preparing you for higher education. Health and science classes, including biology, are very important. Mathematics classes and English classes will help you develop the math, research, and writing skills you will need in college. Because speech-language pathologists and audiologists work so intensely with language, you may also find it beneficial to study a foreign language, paying special attention to how you learn to make sounds and remember words. Speech classes will also improve your awareness of sounds and language and will also improve your speaking and listening skills.

Postsecondary Training

Most states require a master's degree in speech-language pathology or audiology for a beginning job in either profession. Forty-seven states required speech-language pathologists to be licensed if they work in a health care setting, and 12 states require the same license to practice in a public school. Typical majors for those going into this field include communication sciences and disorders, speech and hearing, or education. Regardless of your career goal (speech-language pathologist or audiologist), your undergraduate course work should include classes in anatomy, biology, physiology, physics, and other related areas, such as linguistics, semantics, and phonetics. It is also helpful to have some exposure to child psychology. Accredited graduate programs in speech-language pathology are available from approximately 240 colleges and universities.

To be eligible for certification, which most employers and states require, you must have at least a master's degree from a program accredited by the accreditation council of the American Speech-Language-Hearing Association (ASHA). Currently there are more than 400 programs in speech-language pathology and/or audiology; however, not all of these programs are accredited. It is in your best interest to contact ASHA for a listing of accredited programs before you decide on a graduate school to attend. Accredited graduate programs in speech-language pathology are available at approximately 240 colleges and universities. According to ASHA, as of 2012, audiologists will have to earn a doctorate in order to be certified.

Some schools offer graduate degrees only in speech-language pathology or graduate degrees only in audiology. A number of schools offer degrees in both fields. Graduate-level course work in audiology includes such studies as hearing and language disorders, normal auditory and speech-language development, balance, and audiology instrumentation. Graduate-level work for those in speech-language pathology includes studies in evaluating and treating speech and language disorders, stuttering, pronunciation, and voice modulation. Students of both disciplines are required to complete supervised clinical fieldwork or practicum.

If you plan to go into research, teaching, or administration, you will need to complete a doctorate degree.

Certification or Licensing

To work as a speech pathologist or audiologist in a public school, you will be required to be a certified teacher and you must meet special state requirements if treating children with disabilities. Almost all states regulate audiology and/or speech-language pathology through licensure or title registration, and all but six of those require continuing education for license renewal. In order to become licensed, you must have completed an advanced degree in the field (generally a master's degree, but a doctorate is becoming the new standard for audiologists), pass a standardized test, and complete 300 to 375 hours of supervised clinical experience and nine months of postgraduate professional clinical experience. Some states permit audiologists to dispense hearing aids under an audiology license. Specific education and experience requirements, type of regulation, and title use vary by state.

Many states base their licensing laws on ASHA certification. ASHA offers speech-language pathologists the certificate of clinical competence in speech-language pathology and audiologists the certificate of clinical competence in audiology. To be eligible for these certifications, you must meet certain education requirements, such as the supervised clinical fieldwork experience, and have completed a postgraduate clinical fellowship. The fellowship must be no less than 36 weeks of full-time professional employment or its part-time equivalent. You must then pass an examination in the area in which you want certification.

Other Requirements

Naturally, speech-language pathologists and audiologists should have strong communication skills. Note, though, that this means more than being able to speak clearly. You must be able to explain diagnostic test results and treatment plans in an easily understood way for a variety of clients who are already experiencing problems. As a speech-language pathologist and audiologist, you should enjoy working with people, both your clients and other professionals who may be involved in the client's treatment. In addition, you need patience and compassion. A client's progress may be slow, and you should be supportive and encouraging during these times.

EXPLORING

Although the specialized nature of this work makes it difficult for you to get an informal introduction to either profession, there are opportunities to be found. Official training must begin at the college or university level, but it is possible for you to volunteer in clinics and hospitals. As a prospective speech-language pathologist and audiologist, you may also find it helpful to learn sign language or volunteer your time in speech, language, and hearing centers.

EMPLOYERS

There are approximately 110,000 speech-language pathologists and 12,000 audiologists employed in the United States. About one-half of speech-language pathologists are employed in education, from elementary school to the university level. More than half of all audiologists work in physicians' offices and medical facilities. Other professionals in this field work in state and local governments, hearing aid stores (audiologists), and scientific research facilities. A small but growing number of speech-language pathologists and audiologists are in private practice, generally working with patients referred to them by physicians and other health practitioners.

Some speech-language pathologists and audiologists contract to provide services in schools, hospitals, or nursing homes, or work as consultants to industry.

STARTING OUT

If you want to work in the public school system, your college career services office can help you with interviewing skills. Professors sometimes know of job openings and may even post these openings on a centrally located bulletin board. It may be possible to find employment by contacting a hospital or rehabilitation center. To work in colleges and universities as a specialist in the classroom, clinic, or research center, it is almost mandatory to be working on a graduate degree. Many scholarships, fellowships, and grants for assistants are available in colleges and universities giving courses in speech-language pathology and audiology. Most of these and other assistance programs are offered at the graduate level. The U.S. Rehabilitation Services Administration, the Children's Bureau, the U.S. Department of Education, and the National Institutes of Health allocate funds for teaching and training grants to colleges and universities with graduate study programs. In addition, the Department of Veterans Affairs provides stipends (a fixed allowance) for predoctoral work.

ADVANCEMENT

Advancement in speech-language pathology and audiology is based chiefly on education. Individuals who have completed graduate study will have the best opportunities to enter research and administrative areas, supervising other speech-language pathologists or audiologists either in developmental work or in public school systems.

EARNINGS

The U.S. Department of Labor reports that in 2006 speech-language pathologists earned a median annual salary of $57,710. Salaries ranged from less than $37,970 to more than $90,400. Also in 2006, audiologists earned a median annual salary of $57,120. The lowest 10 percent of these workers earned less than $38,370, while the highest 10 percent earned $89,160 or more per year. Geographic location and type of facility are important salary variables. Almost all employment situations provide fringe benefits such as paid vacations, sick leave, and retirement programs.

WORK ENVIRONMENT

Most speech-language pathologists and audiologists work 40 hours a week at a desk or table in clean, comfortable surroundings. Speech-language pathologists and audiologists who focus on research, however, may work longer hours. The job is not physically demanding but does require attention to detail and intense concentration. The emotional needs of clients and their families may also be demanding.

OUTLOOK

Population growth, lengthening life spans, and increased public awareness of the problems associated with communicative disorders indicate a highly favorable employment outlook for well-qualified personnel. The U.S. Department of Labor predicts that employment for speech-language pathologists and audiologists will grow about as fast as the average for all occupations through 2016. Much of this growth depends on economic factors, further budget cutbacks by health care providers and third-party payers, and legal mandates requiring services for people with disabilities.

Nearly half of the new jobs emerging through the end of the decade are expected to be in speech and hearing clinics, physicians' offices, and outpatient care facilities. Speech-language pathologists and audiologists will be needed in these places, for example, to carry out the increasing number of rehabilitation programs for stroke victims and patients with head injuries.

Substantial job growth will continue to occur in elementary and secondary schools because of the Education for All Handicapped Children Act of 1975 (which was renamed the Individuals with Disabilities Education Act and amended in 1990, 1997, and 2004). This law guarantees special education and related services to minors with disabilities.

Many new jobs will be created in hospitals, nursing homes, rehabilitation centers, and home health agencies; most of these openings will probably be filled by private practitioners employed on a contract basis. Opportunities for speech-language pathologists and audiologists in private practice should increase in the future. There should be a greater demand for consultant audiologists in the area of industrial and environmental noise as manufacturing and other companies develop and carry out noise-control programs. Speech-language pathologists and audiologists who are fluent in a foreign language (such as Spanish) should have especially strong employment prospects.

FOR MORE INFORMATION

The American Auditory Society is concerned with hearing disorders, how to prevent them, and the rehabilitation of individuals with hearing and balance dysfunction.
American Auditory Society
352 Sundial Ridge Circle
Dammeron Valley, UT 84783-5196
Tel: 435-574-0062
http://www.amauditorysoc.org

This professional, scientific, and credentialing association offers information about communication disorders and career and membership information.

American Speech-Language-Hearing Association
2200 Research Boulevard
Rockville, MD 20850-3289
Tel: 800-638-8255
Email: actioncenter@asha.org
http://www.asha.org

This association is for undergraduate and graduate students studying human communication. For information on accredited training programs, news related to the field, and to find out about regional chapters, contact

National Student Speech Language Hearing Association
2200 Research Boulevard
Rockville, MD 20850-3289
Tel: 800-498-2071
Email: nsslha@asha.org
http://www.nsslha.org

Sports Instructors and Coaches

OVERVIEW

Sports instructors demonstrate and explain the skills and rules of particular sports, like golf or tennis, to individuals or groups. They help beginners learn basic rules, stances, grips, movements, and techniques of a game. Sports instructors often help experienced athletes to sharpen their skills.

Coaches work with a single, organized team or individual, teaching the skills associated with that sport. A coach prepares her or his team for competition. During the competition, he or she continues to give instruction from a vantage point near the court or playing field.

HISTORY

Americans have more leisure time than ever and many have decided that they are going to put this time to good use by getting or staying in shape. This fitness boom, as well as a trend toward more sports competitions, has created employment opportunities for many sports-related occupations.

Health clubs, community centers, parks and recreational facilities, and private business now employ sports instructors who teach everything from tennis and golf to scuba diving.

As high school and college sports become even more organized, there continues to be a need for coaches qualified to teach the intricate skills associated with athletics today.

THE JOB

The specific job requirements of sports instructors and coaches vary according to the type of sport and athletes involved. For example, an instructor teaching advanced skiing at a resort in Utah will have different duties and responsibilities than an instructor teaching beginning swimming at a municipal pool. Nevertheless, all instructors and coaches are teachers. They must be very knowledgeable about rules and strategies for their respective sports. They must also have an effective teaching method that reinforces correct techniques and procedures so their students or players will be able to gain from that valuable knowledge. Also, instructors and coaches need to be aware of and open to new procedures and techniques. Many attend clinics or seminars to learn more about their sport or even how to teach more effectively. Many are also members of professional organizations that deal exclusively with their sport.

Safety is a primary concern for all coaches and instructors. Coaches and instructors make sure their students have the right equipment and know its correct use. A major component of safety is helping students feel comfortable and confident with their abilities. This entails teaching the proper stances, techniques, and movements of a game, instructing students on basic rules, and answering any questions.

While instructors may tutor students individually or in small groups, a coach works with all the members of a team. Both use lectures and demonstrations to show students the proper skills, and both point out students' mistakes or deficiencies.

Motivation is another key element in sports instruction. Almost all sports require stamina, and most coaches will tell you that psychological preparation is every bit as important as physical training.

Coaches and instructors also have administrative responsibilities. College coaches actively recruit new players to join their team. Professional coaches attend team meetings with owners and general managers to determine which players they will draft the next season. Sports instructors at health and athletic clubs schedule classes, lessons, and contests.

REQUIREMENTS

Training and educational requirements vary, depending on the specific sport and the ability level of students being instructed. Most coaches who are associated with schools have bachelor's degrees. Many middle and high school coaches are also teachers within the school. Most instructors need to combine several years of successful experience in a particular sport with some educational background, preferably in teaching. A college degree is becoming more important as part of an instructor's background.

High School

To prepare for college courses, high school students should take courses that teach human physiology. Biology, health, and exercise classes would all be helpful. Courses in English and speech are also important to improve or develop communication skills.

There is no substitute for developing expertise in a sport. If you can play the sport well and effectively explain to other people how they might play, you will most likely be able to get a job as a sports instructor. The most significant source of training for this occupation is gained while on the job.

Postsecondary Training

Postsecondary training in this field varies greatly. College and professional coaches often attended college as athletes, while others attended college and received their degrees without playing a sport. If you are interested in becoming a high school coach, you will need a college degree because you will most likely be teaching as well as coaching. At the high school level, coaches spend their days teaching everything from physical education to English to mathematics, and so the college courses these coaches take vary greatly. Coaches of some youth league sports may not need a postsecondary degree, but they must have a solid understanding of their sport and of injury prevention.

Certification or Licensing

Many facilities require sports instructors to be certified. Information on certification is available from any organization that deals with the specific sport in which one might be interested.

Since most high school coaches also work as teachers, those interested in this job should plan to obtain teacher certification in their state.

Other Requirements

Coaches have to be experts in their sport. They must have complete knowledge of the rules and strategies of the game, so that they can creatively design effective plays and techniques for their athletes. But the requirements for this job do not end here. Good coaches are able to communicate their extensive knowledge to the athletes in a way that not only instructs the athletes, but also inspires them to perform to their fullest potential. Therefore, coaches are also teachers.

"I think I'm good at my job because I love working with people and because I'm disciplined in everything I do," says Dawn Shannahan, former assistant girls' basketball and track coach at Leyden

High School in Franklin Park, Illinois. Discipline is important for athletes, as they must practice plays and techniques over and over again. Coaches who cannot demonstrate and encourage this type of discipline will have difficulty helping their athletes improve. Shannahan adds, "I've seen coaches who are really knowledgeable about their sport but who aren't patient enough to allow for mistakes or for learning." Patience can make all the difference between an effective coach and one who is unsuccessful.

Similarly, Shannahan says, "A coach shouldn't be a pessimist. The team could be losing by a lot, but you have to stay optimistic and encourage the players." Coaches must be able to work under pressure, guiding teams through games and tournaments that carry great personal and possibly financial stakes for everyone involved.

EXPLORING

Try to gain as much experience as possible in all sports and a specific sport in particular. It is never too early to start. High school and college offer great opportunities to participate in sporting events either as a player, manager, trainer, or in intramural leagues.

Most communities have sports programs such as Little League baseball or track and field meets sponsored by a recreation commission. Get involved by volunteering as a coach, umpire, or starter.

Talking with sports instructors already working in the field is also a good way to discover specific job information and find out about career opportunities.

EMPLOYERS

Besides working in high schools, coaches are hired by colleges and universities, professional sports teams, individual athletes such as tennis players, and by youth leagues, summer camps, and recreation centers.

STARTING OUT

People with expertise in a particular sport, who are interested in becoming an instructor, should apply directly to the appropriate facility. Sometimes a facility will provide training.

For those interested in coaching, many colleges offer positions to *graduate assistant coaches*. Graduate assistant coaches are recently graduated players who are interested in becoming coaches. They receive a stipend and gain valuable coaching experience.

ADVANCEMENT

Advancement opportunities for both instructors and coaches depend on the individual's skills, willingness to learn, and work ethic. A sports instructor's success can be measured by their students' caliber of play and the number of students they instruct. Successful instructors may become well known enough to open their own schools or camps, write books, or produce how-to videos.

Some would argue that a high percentage of wins is the only criteria for success for professional coaches. However, coaches in the scholastic ranks have other responsibilities and other factors that measure success; for example, high school and college coaches must make sure their players are getting good grades. All coaches must try to produce a team that competes in a sportsmanlike fashion regardless of whether they win or lose.

Successful coaches are often hired by larger schools. High school coaches may advance to become college coaches, and the most successful college coaches often are given the opportunity to coach professional teams. Former players sometimes land assistant or head coaching positions.

EARNINGS

Earnings for sports instructors and coaches vary considerably depending on the sport and the person or team being coached. The coach of a Wimbledon champion commands much more money per hour than the swimming instructor for the tadpole class at the municipal pool.

The U.S. Department of Labor reports that the median earnings for sports coaches and instructors were $26,950 in 2006. The lowest 10 percent earned less than $13,990, while the highest 10 percent earned more than $58,890. Sports instructors and coaches who worked at colleges and universities earned a mean annual salary of $44,200 in 2006, while those employed by elementary and secondary schools earned $27,550.

Much of the work is part time, and part-time employees generally do not receive paid vacations, sick days, or health insurance. Instructors who teach group classes for beginners through park districts or at city recreation centers can expect to earn around $6 per hour. An hour-long individual lesson through a golf course or tennis club averages $75. Many times, coaches for children's teams work as volunteers.

Many sports instructors work in camps teaching swimming, archery, sailing and other activities. These instructors generally earn between $1,000 and $2,500, plus room and board, for a summer session.

Full-time fitness instructors at gyms or health clubs earned salaries that ranged from less than $14,880 to $56,750 or more per year in 2006, with a median salary of $25,910, according to the U.S. Department of Labor. Instructors with many years of experience and a college degree have the highest earning potential.

Most coaches who work at the high school level or below also teach within the school district. Besides their teaching salary and coaching fee—either a flat rate or a percentage of their annual salary—school coaches receive a benefits package that includes paid vacations and health insurance.

Head college football coaches at NCAA Division I schools earned an average of $950,000 a year in 2006, according to *USA Today*. A few top football coaches earn more than $2 million annually. Some top coaches in men's Division I basketball earn salaries of $1 million or more, according to *USA Today*. Women's basketball coaches at the college level typically earn lower salaries than their colleagues who coach men's sports—although top coaches earn salaries that are on par with coaches of men's basketball teams.

Coaches for professional teams often earn between $200,000 and $3 million a year. Some top coaches can earn more than $5 million annually. Many popular coaches augment their salaries with fees obtained from personal appearances and endorsements.

WORK ENVIRONMENT

An instructor or coach may work indoors, in a gym or health club, or outdoors, perhaps at a swimming pool. Much of the work is part time. Full-time sports instructors generally work between 35 and 40 hours per week. During the season when their teams compete, coaches can work 16 hours each day, five or six days each week.

It is not unusual for coaches or instructors to work evenings or weekends. Instructors work then because that is when their adult students are available for instruction. Coaches work nights and weekends because those are the times their teams compete.

One significant drawback to this job is the lack of job security. A club may hire a new instructor on very little notice, or may cancel a scheduled class for lack of interest. Athletic teams routinely fire coaches after losing seasons.

Sports instructors and coaches should enjoy working with a wide variety of people. They should be able to communicate clearly and possess good leadership skills to effectively teach complex skills. They can take pride in the knowledge that they have helped their students or their players reach new heights of achievement and training.

OUTLOOK

Americans' interest in health, physical fitness, and body image continues to send people to gyms and playing fields. This fitness boom has created strong employment opportunities for many people in sports-related occupations.

Health clubs, community centers, parks and recreational facilities, and private business now employ sports instructors who teach everything from tennis and golf to scuba diving.

According to the U.S. Department of Labor, these careers will grow faster than the average for all occupations through 2016. Job opportunities will be best in high schools and in amateur athletic leagues. Health clubs, adult education programs, and private industry will require competent, dedicated instructors. Those with the most training, education, and experience will have the best chance for employment.

The creation of new professional leagues, as well as the expansion of current leagues, will open some new employment opportunities for professional coaches, but competition for these jobs will be very intense. There will also be openings as other coaches retire, or are terminated. However, there is very little job security in coaching, unless a coach can consistently produce a winning team.

FOR MORE INFORMATION

For certification information, trade journals, job listings, and a list of graduate schools, visit the AAHPERD's Web site.

American Alliance for Health, Physical Education, Recreation and Dance (AAHPERD)
1900 Association Drive
Reston, VA 20191-1598
Tel: 800-213-7193
http://www.aahperd.org

For information on membership and baseball coaching education, coaching Web links, and job listings, visit the ABCA's Web site.

American Baseball Coaches Association (ABCA)
108 South University Avenue, Suite 3
Mount Pleasant, MI 48858-2327
Tel: 989-775-3300
Email: abca@abca.org
http://www.abca.org

For information on football coaching careers, contact
American Football Coaches Association
100 Legends Lane
Waco, TX 76706-1243
Tel: 254-754-9900
Email: info@afca.com
http://www.afca.com

For informational on hockey coaching, contact
American Hockey Coaches Association
7 Concord Street
Gloucester, MA 01930-2300
Tel: 781-245-4177
http://www.ahcahockey.com

For information on careers in sports and physical education, contact
National Association for Sport and Physical Education
1900 Association Drive
Reston, VA 20191-1598
Tel: 800-213-7193
Email: naspe@aahperd.org
http://www.aahperd.org/naspe

For information on basketball coaching, contact
National Association of Basketball Coaches
1111 Main Street, Suite 1000
Kansas City, MO 64105-2136
Tel: 816-878-6222
http://nabc.cstv.com

For information on high school coaching opportunities, contact
National High School Athletic Coaches Association
PO Box 10065
Fargo, ND 58106-0065
Email: office@hscoaches.org
http://www.hscoaches.org

For information on the coaching of soccer, contact
National Soccer Coaches Association of America
6700 Squibb Road, Suite 215
Mission, KS 66202-3252
Tel: 800-458-0678
http://www.nscaa.com

For information on women's basketball coaching, contact
Women's Basketball Coaches Association
4646 Lawrenceville Highway
Lilburn, GA 30047-3620
Tel: 770-279-8027
Email: wbca@wbca.org
http://www.wbca.org

Teacher Aides

OVERVIEW

Teacher aides perform a wide variety of duties to help teachers run a classroom. Teacher aides prepare instructional materials, help students with classroom work, and supervise students in the library, on the playground, and at lunch. They perform administrative duties such as photocopying, keeping attendance records, and grading papers. There are approximately 1.3 million teacher aides employed in the United States.

HISTORY

As formal education became more widely available in the 20th century, teachers' jobs became more complex. The size of classes increased, and a growing educational bureaucracy demanded that more records be kept of students' achievements and classroom activities. Advancements in technology, changes in educational theory, and an increase in the amount and variety of available teaching materials all called for more time to prepare materials and assess student progress, leaving teachers less time for teaching.

To remedy this problem, teacher aides began to be employed to take care of the more routine aspects of running an instructional program. Today, many schools and school districts employ teacher aides, to the great benefit of hardworking teachers and students.

THE JOB

Teacher aides work in public, private, and parochial preschools and elementary and secondary schools. Their duties vary depending on the classroom teacher, school, and school district. Some teacher aides specialize in one subject, and some work in a specific type of school setting. These settings include bilingual classrooms, gifted and talented programs, classes for learning disabled students and those with unique physical needs, and multi-age classrooms. These aides conduct the same type of classroom work as other teacher aides, but they may provide more individual assistance to students.

Fran Moker works as a teacher aide in a dropout prevention unit at a middle school. Her work involves enrolling students in the unit and explaining the program to parents. She maintains files on the students and attends to other administrative duties. "I work directly with the sixth, seventh, and eighth grade teachers," Moker says, "making all the copies, setting up conferences, and grading papers. I also cover their classes when necessary for short periods of time to give the teachers a break." She also works directly with students, tutoring and advising. "I listen to students when they have problems," she says. "We work with at-risk students, so it's necessary to be supportive. Many of our students come from broken homes and have parents with serious drug and alcohol problems. Consistent caring is a must."

No matter what kind of classroom they assist in, teacher aides will likely copy, compile, and hand out class materials, set up and operate audiovisual equipment, arrange field trips, and type or word-process materials. They organize classroom files, including grade reports, attendance, and health records. They may also obtain library materials and order classroom supplies.

Teacher aides may be in charge of keeping order in classrooms, school cafeterias, libraries, hallways, and playgrounds. Often, they wait with preschool and elementary students coming to or leaving school and make sure all students are accounted for. When a class leaves its room for such subjects as art, music, physical education, or computer lab, teacher aides may go with the students to help the teachers of these other subjects.

Another responsibility of teacher aides is correcting and grading homework and tests, usually for objective assignments and tests that require specific answers. They use answer sheets to mark students' papers and examinations and keep records of students' scores. In some large schools, an aide may be called a *grading clerk* and be responsible only for scoring objective tests and computing and recording test scores. Often using an electronic grading machine or computer, the grading clerk totals errors and computes the percentage of questions answered correctly. The worker then records this

Mean Annual Earnings By Industry, 2006

Educational Support Services	$26,740
Junior Colleges	$26,360
Colleges, Universities, and Professional Schools	$26,200
Elementary and Secondary Schools	$21,890
Individual and Family Services	$20,760
Child Day Care Services	$18,840

Source: U.S. Department of Labor

score and averages students' test scores to determine their grade for the course.

Under the teacher's supervision, teacher aides may work directly with students in the classroom. They listen to a group of young students read aloud or involve the class in a special project such as a science fair, art project, or drama production. With older students, teacher aides provide review or study sessions prior to exams or give extra help with research projects or homework. Some teacher aides work with individual students in a tutorial setting, helping in areas of special need or concern. They may work with the teacher to prepare lesson plans, bibliographies, charts, or maps. They may help to decorate the classroom, design bulletin boards and displays, and arrange workstations. Teacher aides may even participate in parent–teacher conferences to discuss students' progress.

REQUIREMENTS

High School

Courses in English, history, social studies, mathematics, art, drama, physical education, and the sciences will provide you with a broad base of knowledge. This knowledge will enable you to help students learn in these same subjects. Knowledge of a second language can be an asset, especially when working in schools with bilingual student, parent, or staff populations. Courses in child care, home economics, and psychology are also valuable for this career. You should try to gain some experience working with computers; students at many elementary schools and even preschools now do a large amount of computer work, and computer skills are important in performing clerical duties.

Postsecondary Training

Postsecondary requirements for teacher aides depend on the school or school district and the kinds of responsibilities the aides have. In districts where aides perform mostly clerical duties, applicants may need only to have a high school diploma or the equivalent, Graduation Equivalency Diploma (GED). Those who work in the classroom may be required to take some college courses and attend in-service training and special teacher conferences and seminars. Some schools and districts may help you pay some of the costs involved in attending these programs. Often community and junior colleges have certificate and associate's programs that prepare teacher aides for classroom work, offering courses in child development, health and safety, and child guidance.

Newly hired aides participate in orientation sessions and formal training at the school. In these sessions, aides learn about the school's organization, operation, and philosophy. They learn how to keep school records, operate audiovisual equipment, check books out of the library, and administer first aid.

Many schools prefer to hire teacher aides who have some experience working with children; some schools prefer to hire workers who live within the school district. Schools may also require that you pass written exams and health physicals. You must be able to work effectively with both children and adults and should have good verbal and written communication skills.

Other Requirements

You must enjoy working with children and be able to handle their demands, problems, and questions with patience and fairness. You must be willing and able to follow instructions, but you also should be able to take initiative in projects. Flexibility, creativity, and a cheerful outlook are definite assets for anyone working with children. You should find out the specific job requirements from the school, school district, or state department of education in the area where you would like to work. Requirements vary from school to school and state to state. It is important to remember that an aide who is qualified to work in one state, or even one school, may not be qualified to work in another.

EXPLORING

You can gain experience working with children by volunteering to help with religious education classes at your place of worship. You may volunteer to help with scouting troops or work as a counselor at a summer camp. You may have the opportunity to volunteer to help coach a children's athletic team or work with children in after-school programs at community centers. Babysitting is a common way to gain experience in working with children and to learn about the different stages of child development.

EMPLOYERS

Approximately 1.3 million workers are employed as teacher assistants in the United States. Nearly 40 percent of teacher assistants work part time. With the national shortage of teachers, aides can find work in just about any preschool, elementary, or secondary school in the country. Teacher aides also assist in special education programs and in group home settings. Aides work in both public and private schools.

STARTING OUT

You can apply directly to schools and school districts for teacher aide positions. Many school districts and state departments of education maintain job listings, bulletin boards, and hotlines that list available job openings. Teacher aide jobs are often advertised in the classified section of the newspaper. Once you are hired as a teacher aide, you will spend the first months in special training and will receive a beginning wage. After six months or so, you'll have regular responsibilities and possibly a wage increase.

ADVANCEMENT

Teacher aides usually advance only in terms of increases in salary or responsibility, which come with experience. Aides in some districts may receive time off to take college courses. Some teacher aides choose to pursue bachelor's degrees and fulfill the licensing requirements of the state or school to become teachers. "I will probably always remain in the education field," Fran Moker says, "maybe someday returning to school to get a degree in education."

Some aides, who find that they enjoy the administrative side of the job, may move into school or district office staff positions. Others choose to get more training and then work as resource teachers, tutors, guidance counselors, or reading, mathematics, or speech specialists. Some teacher aides go into school library work or become media specialists. While it is true that most of these jobs require additional training, the job of teacher aide is a good place to begin.

EARNINGS

Teacher aides are usually paid on an hourly basis and usually only during the nine or 10 months of the school calendar. Salaries vary depending on the school or district, region of the country, and the duties the aides perform. Median annual earnings of teacher assistants were $20,740 in 2006, according to the U.S. Department of Labor. Salaries ranged from less than $13,910 to more than $31,610.

Benefits such as health insurance and vacation or sick leave may also depend on the school or district as well as the number of hours a teacher aide works. Many schools employ teacher aides only part time and do not offer such benefits. Other teacher aides may receive the same health and pension benefits as the teachers in their school and be covered under collective bargaining agreements.

WORK ENVIRONMENT

Teacher aides work in a well-lit, comfortable, wheelchair-accessible environment, although some older school buildings may be in disrepair with unpredictable heating or cooling systems. Most of their work will be indoors, but teacher aides will spend some time outside before and after school, and during recess and lunch hours, to watch over the students. They are often on their feet, monitoring the halls and lunch areas and running errands for teachers. Although this work is not physically strenuous, working closely with children can be stressful and tiring.

Teacher aides find it rewarding to help students learn and develop. The pay, however, is not as rewarding. "As with all those in the entire education field," Fran Moker says, "we are grossly underpaid. But that's the only negative. I truly enjoy my job." Because of her commitment to her work, Fran is allowed certain benefits, such as time off when needed.

OUTLOOK

The U.S. Department of Labor predicts that this field will grow by 10 percent between 2006 and 2016—or about as fast as the average for all occupations. The field of special education (working with students with specific learning, emotional, or physical concerns or disabilities) is expected to grow rapidly, and more aides will be needed in these areas.

Several other factors should spur growth in this field. A shortage of teachers will cause administrators to hire more aides to help with larger classrooms. Additionally, teacher aides will play an increasing role in preparing students for standardized testing, helping students who perform poorly academically, and assisting students for whom English is a second language.

Teacher aides who want to work with young children in day care or extended day programs will have a relatively easy time finding work because more children are attending these programs while their parents are at work. Because of increased responsibilities for aides, state departments of education will likely establish standards of training.

Teacher aides who have at least two years of postsecondary experience, are experienced with working with special education students, and who are fluent in a foreign language will have the best employment prospects.

FOR MORE INFORMATION

To learn about current issues affecting paraprofessionals in education, contact the following organizations:

American Federation of Teachers (AFT)
555 New Jersey Avenue, NW
Washington, DC 20001-2029
Tel: 202-879-4400
Email: online@aft.org
http://www.aft.org

National Education Association
1201 16th Street, NW
Washington, DC 20036-3290
Tel: 202-833-4000
http://www.nea.org

To order publications or read current research and other information, contact

Association for Childhood Education International
17904 Georgia Avenue, Suite 215
Olney, MD 20832-2277
Tel: 800-423-3563
Email: headquarters@acei.org
http://www.acei.org

For information about training programs and other resources, contact

National Resource Center for Paraprofessionals
Tel: 435-797-7272
Email: info@nrcpara.org
http://www.nrcpara.org

Index